SALT WATER SPORTFISHING TECHNIQUES

MARK SOSIN
AND
GEORGE POVEROMO

OUTDOOR ASSOCIATES
BOOKS

Published by
OUTDOOR ASSOCIATES, INC.
9930 N.W. 59th Court
Parkland, Florida 33076

PRINTED IN THE UNITED STATES OF AMERICA
ISBN 0-945443-01-3

*A special thank you to George Volpe and the entire Supertype Crew for their hard work,
determination and professionalism in readying this publication for printing.*

CONTENTS

FIELDING A FISHING BOAT
1

PUTTING THE OUTFIT TOGETHER
9

RIGGING AND FISHING ARTIFICIALS
13

THE MAGIC MOMENT
19

CATCHING FISH WITH ELECTRONICS
25

THE END OF THE LINE
31

BAIT RIGGING
41

AS THE TIDE TURNS
47

THE TRIPLE THREAT
53

APPROACH AND PRESENTATION
59

GETTING STARTED IN SALT WATER FLY FISHING
65

INSIDER'S LOOK AT OFFSHORE FISHING
69

TRAILERING KNOW-HOW
75

FINDING FISH
81

COVERS
Carey Chen of Miami, Florida, is an extremely talented artist specializing in marine paintings. His attention to detail, a thorough knowledge of the sport and a natural ability enable him to create life-like illustrations that are in demand nationwide. These offshore and inshore gamefish were painted especially for the National Seminar Series.
Contact: Arts by Carey, (305) 386-4378.

ILLUSTRATIONS
David McHose is the staff illustrator for Salt Water Sportsman Magazine. His work has appeared in numerous marine industry advertisements, catalogs and books. He also specializes in limited edition fish prints and has recently introduced a line of Catch and Release Prints. A resident of Deerfield Beach, Florida, Dave can be reached at (305) 421-0832.

ABOUT THE AUTHORS

An award-winning writer, photographer, and television producer, **MARK SOSIN** has an impressive list of credits that span virtually all phases of outdoor communication. He is the Producer and on-camera host of Mark Sosin's Saltwater Journal on ESPN. More than 2,500 of his articles have been published in major magazines and he has written 24 books on the outdoors. He has fished extensively for most major gamefish in 40 countries on five continents.

Sosin is a Past President of the Outdoor Writers Association of America and recipient of its coveted Excellence In Craft Award as well as its prestigious Ham Brown Award. He has been voted into both the International Fishing Hall of Fame and the Freshwater Fishing Hall of Fame. Professional memberships include the American Society of Journalists and Authors, Society of Professional Journalists, and the Southeast Outdoor Press Association.

GEORGE POVEROMO is a nationally recognized and well respected sportfishing expert. His in-depth knowledge of marine angling and its techniques is the result of an insatiable passion for fishing that developed at an early age. Poveromo has fished along the entire U.S. coast, as well as in Alaska, Hawaii, Bermuda, Mexico and the Baja, the Bahamas chain and numerous Caribbean, central and south American destinations. As Salt Water Sportsman's Field Editor, he continues his world-wide pursuit of gamefish. His strong background in boating is also reflected in a monthly column for the magazine, and by his demand as a consultant for several major marine manufacturers.

Poveromo is an active member of the Outdoor Writers Association of America, Southeast Outdoor Press Association, and Boating Writers International.

Water Temperature Ranges for Salt Water Fish

The table lists water temperatures applicable to many of the more popular salt water game fish species. Under the *Lower* heading are temperatures which a particular species tends to avoid, although it might swim through water colder than that indicated. Similarly, under *Upper* are temperatures which the fish normally shun. The *Range* column lists temperature limits which are most favorable for angling.

Both Fahrenheit (F) & Celsius (C) readings are given since water temperatures obtained from governmental satellites normally are given in the latter only.

Note that ocean surface water temperatures may vary considerably from those at greater depths and such variations should be taken into account when actually fishing. Thus a tilefish, feeding in 500 feet of water ranging around 55°F, may be found when the surface is well above that temperature.

SPECIES	LOWER	UPPER	RANGE
Albacore	59°F	67°F	62°-65°F
(Thunnus alalunga)	15°C	19°C	16°-18°C
Amberjack	60°F	72°F	63°-67°F
(Seriola dumerili)	16°C	22°C	17°-19°C
Barracuda, Atlantic	65°F	90°F	75°-85°F
(Sphyraena barracuda)	18°C	32°C	24°-29°C
Barracuda, Pacific	54°F	71°F	64°-67°F
(Sphyraena argentia)	12°C	22°C	18°-19°C
Bass, Black Sea	48°F	85°F	60°-70°F
(Centropristes striatus)	9°C	29°C	16°-21°C
Bass, Kelp	62°F	73°F	65°-68°F
(Paralabrax clathratus)	16°C	23°C	18°-20°C
Bass, Striped	40°F	80°F	45°-65°F
(Morone saxatilis)	5°C	27°C	7°-18°C
Bass, White Sea	58°F	75°F	65°-69°F
(Cynoscion nobilis)	14°C	23°C	18°-21°C
Bluefish	50°F	84°F	62°-70°F
(Pomatomus saltatrix)	10°C	29°C	18°-21°C
Bonefish	68°F	90°F	72°-82°F
(Albula vulpes)	20°C	32°C	22°-27°C
Bonito, Atlantic	57°F	72°F	63°-67°F
(Sarda sarda)	14°C	22°C	16°-19°C
Bonito, Pacific	59°F	74°F	64°-68°F
(Sarda chiliensis)	15°C	23°C	18°-20°C
Cobia	55°F	82°F	66°-72°F
(Rachycentron canadus)	12°C	27°C	19°-22°C
Cod	32°F	59°F	44°-49°F
(Gadus morhua)	0°C	15°C	6°- 8°C
Croaker	41°F	85°F	60°-70°F
(Micropogon undulatus)	5°C	29°C	16°-21°C
Dolphin	69°F	80°F	73°-77°F
(Coryphaena hippurus)	21°C	27°C	23°-25°C
Drum, Black	55°F	90°F	68°-74°F
(Pogonias cromis)	12°C	32°C	20°-23°C
Drum, Red (Channel Bass)	59°F	85°F	69°-73°F
(Sciaenops ocellata)	15°C	29°C	21°-23°C
Flounder, Summer (Fluke)	69°F	80°F	73°-77°F
(Paralichthys dentatus)	21°C	27°C	23°-25°C
Flounder, Winter	35°F	60°F	48°-52°F
(Pseudopleuronectes americanus)	2°C	16°C	9°-11°C
Haddock	36°F	52°F	45°-50°F
(Melanogramus aeglefinus)	2°C	11°C	7°- 9°C
Jack Crevalle	65°F	85°F	70°-78°F
(Caranx hippos)	18°C	29°C	21°-25°C
Mackerel, Atlantic	45°F	70°F	60°-65°F
(Scomber scrombrus)	7°C	21°C	18°-20°C
Mackerel, King	70°F	88°F	74°-79°F
(Scomberomorus cavalla)	21°C	31°C	23°-26°C
Mackerel, Pacific	47°F	70°F	56°-62°F
(Pneumatophorus diego)	9°C	21°C	13°-16°C
Mackerel, Spanish	68°F	85°F	72°-80°F
(Scomberomorus maculatus)	20°C	29°C	22°-27°C
Marlin, Black	70°F	87°F	75°-79°F
(Makaira indicus)	21°C	30°C	24°-26°C

SPECIES	LOWER	UPPER	RANGE
Marlin, Blue	69°F	88°F	75°-80°F
(Makaira nigricans)	21°C	31°C	24°-27°C
Marlin, Striped	61°F	78°F	68°-72°F
(Tetrapturus audax)	16°C	25°C	20°-22°C
Marlin, White	62°F	84°F	66°-76°F
(Tetrapturus albidus)	16°C	29°C	19°-24°C
Permit	67°F	85°F	70°-78°F
(Trachinotus falcatus)	19°C	29°C	21°-25°C
Pollock	33°F	60°F	44°-50°F
(Pollachius virens)	1°C	15°C	6°-10°C
Pompano	68°F	85°F	75°-80°F
(Trachinotus cardinus)	20°C	29°C	21°-25°C
Sailfish	70°F	88°F	76°-81°F
(Istiophorus platyperus)	21°C	31°C	24°-27°C
Scup (Porgy)	42°F	73°F	57°-64°F
(Stenotomus versicolor)	6°C	23°C	14°-18°C
Seatrout (Spotted Weakfish)	62°F	90°F	70°-75°F
(Cynoscion nebulosus)	16°C	32°C	21°-23°C
Shark, Blue	55°F	73°F	60°-68°F
(Prionace glauca)	12°C	23°C	15°-20°C
Shark, Mako	60°F	78°F	65°-72°F
(Isurus oxyrinchus)	15°C	25°C	18°-22°C
Sheepshead	60°F	78°F	65°-72°F
(Archosargus probatocephalus)	15°C	25°C	18°-22°C
Snapper, Red	50°F	64°F	55°-60°F
(Lutjanus campechanus)	10°C	18°C	13°-16°C
Snook	62°F	90°F	75°-85°F
(Centropomus undecimalis)	16°C	32°C	23°-30°C
Spot	60°F	95°F	70°-80°F
(Leiostomus xanthurus)	15°C	35°C	21°-27°C
Swordfish	50°F	78°F	64°-68°F
(Xiphias gladius)	10°C	25°C	18°-20°C
Tarpon	72°F	90°F	75°-85°F
(Megalops atlantica)	22°C	32°C	24°-30°C
Tautog (Blackfish)	60°F	76°F	68°-72°F
(Tautoga onitis)	16°C	24°C	20°-22°C
Tilefish	48°F	59°F	50°-57°F
(Lopholatilus chamaeleonticeps)	9°C	15°C	10°-14°C
Tuna, Bigeye	55°F	68°F	60°-65°F
(Thunnus obesus)	13°C	20°C	15°-18°C
Tuna, Blackfin	70°F	82°F	72°-79°F
(Thunnus atlanticus)	21°C	27°C	22°-26°C
Tuna, Bluefin	50°F	82°F	61°-67°F
(Thunnus thynnus)	10°C	27°C	16°-19°C
Tuna, Skipjack	55°F	75°F	60°-70°F
Euthynnus pelamis)	13°C	23°C	15°-21°C
Tuna, Yellowfin	60°F	80°F	73°-77°F
(Thunnus albacares)	15°C	27°C	23°-25°C
Wahoo	68°F	85°F	72°-80°F
(Ancanthocybium solandri)	20°C	29°C	22°-27°C
Weakfish	55°F	78°F	68°-71°F
(Cynoscion regalis)	13°C	25°C	20°-22°C
Yellowtail, Pacific	60°F	72°F	64°-68°F
(Seriola dorsalis)	15°C	22°C	18°-20°C

Courtesy: Hal Lyman, Salt Water Sportsman

A boat should support your style of fishing. Notice the clean and unobstructed layout of this center console, its rod capacity, fighting chair and rocket launcher.

1 FIELDING A FISHING BOAT

Choosing and rigging a fishing boat is exciting. Whether you're a seasoned veteran or a novice there's a certain euphoria that goes with determining what type of equipment to purchase and how to set it up for maximum fish-ability. While such a quest may seem like old hat to serious anglers, a newcomer is often baffled and even intimated over deciding on his exact needs.

The most important factor, outside of budget, is acquiring a boat which best suits your immediate fishing needs. Consider the type of fishing you do most. If bays and sounds account for most of the effort, the fuel efficiency of a modified-V hull design may be a practical choice, or even a specialized flats skiff if extreme shallows are frequented. Conversely, if one's sport beckons him offshore or across major open water stretches, the smooth, wave-slicing characteristics of a deep-V hull make it a safe and seaworthy decision.

Fuel capacities also rate right up there. Factor in the fishing distances routinely traveled, engine size, and how much fuel the hull holds, adding in a fuel surplus as a cushion for rough water, extra distances and hard running. Check into fish boxes. Can they sufficiently accommodate the quarry the boat's intended for? Are they insulated and have adequate drainage for melted ice and slush to preserve the quality of the catch, eliminating the need for an aftermarket macerator and plumbing work? They're all considerations that make the difference between a good boat and an excellent one, items which also enhance resale value.

Center consoles are formidable fishing machines. Their design provides 360 degrees of relatively unobstructed room,

which means plenty of space for casting, jigging, live baiting and trolling. The choice of the most dedicated small boat anglers, they're just as proficient trading licks with the million dollar sportfishing yachts many miles offshore as they are running the beaches. Most models have more than adequate fuel capacities and are quality-built to handle challenging sea conditions.

Their obvious drawback is just that: a serious fishing

Speed, fish-ability and generous fuel capacities are non-negotiable to the serious angler. Center consoles are no-nonsense fishing machines, but sometimes a cuddy-cabin or a full weather enclosure may be a more practical choice for the family.

machine. If there's family participation a buyer may be better off with the extra amenities provided by a cuddy version. The shade, comfort, showers and heads available on many models will be a big hit among the family, and probably with yourself on those overnight jaunts. Boat builders are placing more emphasis on designing the ultimate walk-around cuddy and their current products are not only attractive but the perfect compromise for the hard-core, family oriented angler.

The extra cockpit space preserved by a full transom is a big benefit for both the family and angler. Mounting the outboards on a bracket or platform extending from a full transom also provides an enclosed cockpit, a psychological plus when carrying small children. Exactly which design is best (full or notched) is a matter of personal opinion. Traditionalists claim the notched version keeps the outboards in close and supported by the buoyancy of the transom, respectively reducing the risk of a cut-off if a fish surges toward them and submersion or direct spray while underway. Proponents of the full transom believe an adept boat handler can "quarter" a large fish to the gaff, never letting it get near the power, and that the better transom platforms offer enough buoyancy to shield engines from the elements.

SCRUTINIZE THE PLATFORM

Whether rigging out a new boat or modifying an older model, the platform should be able to support your style of fishing. If the boat is used primarily for trolling, position the permanent gunwale holders to where the ones intended for the flat lines angle directly off the stern (keeping them close to the cockpit if the gunwales are wide enough) while those designated for the outriggers should angle about 45 degrees outboard (sinking them as close to the outside gunwales as possible). By angling and offsetting the holders meant for the outrigger rods there is less chance of the fishing line coming taught across a flat line. This same set-up enables four lines to be trolled behind small skiffs lacking outriggers. A pair of outrigger clips fastened to the transom eyes enhance the attractiveness of the flat lines by reducing the angle at which they enter the water. If there's a problem with a bait or lure skipping across a bumpy sea or if you want a bait to ride just below the surface, run the fishing line through the clip. Again, this trick changes the angle of the flat lines, helping separate them from the far ones fished without outriggers. You might consider gunwale mounting another pair of rod holders at a 90 degree angle forward of the primary four or fastening them to the bowrail. They'll come in handy when drifting.

With a little planning, it's not difficult to deploy several trolling outfits from a small boat. Part of the formula requires outriggers, transom clips and either a rocket launcher or a fighting chair with rod holders.

It doesn't make much sense to invest in a boat that can't handle the fish you pursue most. Check fishbox for size, insulation and adequate drainage.

Building rod storage into a boat calls for custom holders. A rocket launcher is a tool that keeps your most important fishing rods highly accessible.

Creating additional rod storage is no problem with custom rod racks and a rocket launcher. Special vertical racks that keep fishing rods handy on both sides of the console (on an open boat), or nearby, increase storage and an angler's potential to catch fish; you'll have quick access to any one of an assortment of rods rigged to cover a variety of situations without fumbling to recover it from beneath the gunwales or within the cuddy. The vertical holders are also ideal for storing rods quickly and easily when clearing the deck to fight a fish. And when it's time to resume fishing the gear can be sorted out and deployed quickly. Under-the-gunwale racks, great for transporting tackle to and from the fishing grounds, are fine in a pinch providing they have the depth and width to facilitate quick deployment.

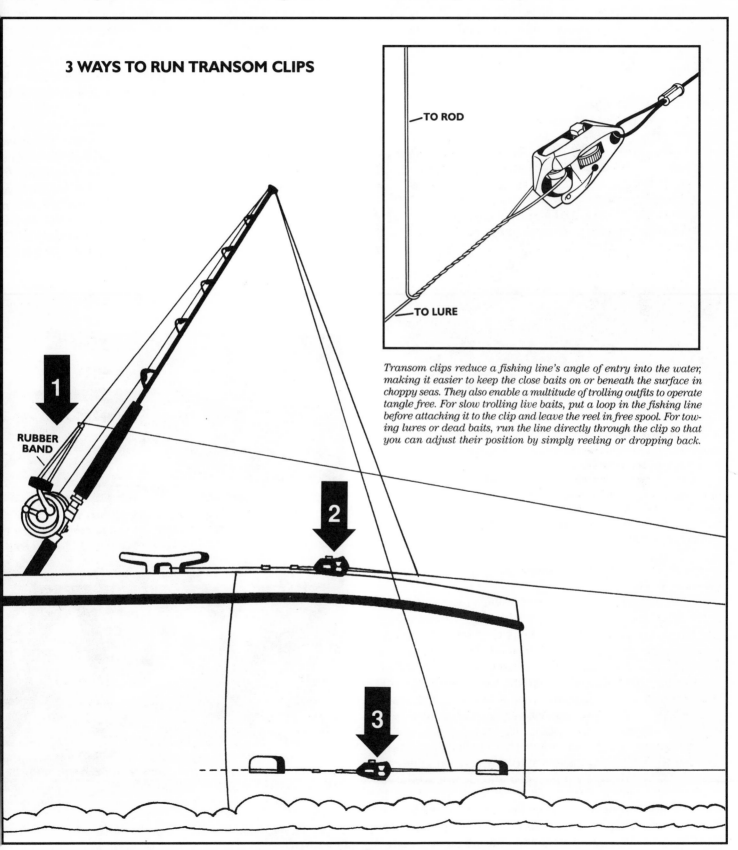

3 WAYS TO RUN TRANSOM CLIPS

TO ROD

TO LURE

RUBBER BAND

Transom clips reduce a fishing line's angle of entry into the water, making it easier to keep the close baits on or beneath the surface in choppy seas. They also enable a multitude of trolling outfits to operate tangle free. For slow trolling live baits, put a loop in the fishing line before attaching it to the clip and leave the reel in free spool. For towing lures or dead baits, run the line directly through the clip so that you can adjust their position by simply reeling or dropping back.

LIVE WELLS:

There's more emphasis now on live baiting than ever before, a trend that's guaranteed to blossom in the years ahead. It's a deadly technique because it presents a live bait to a gamefish in an open environment. Whereas it takes a certain amount of finesse (and hunger on the fish's part) to coax a strike on an artificial or dead, natural bait, the frantic motions and distress vibrations emitted by a live bait suspended in a hostile neighborhood has pushed even the most suspecting gamefish over the edge time and time again! Fur-

A quality deep cycle battery is a fisherman's best friend. They have the cranking amps to turn over marine power and support numerous accessories such as live wells, trolling motors, down-riggers, spreader lights, etc. They can be drawn down and fully recharged over 400 times without sapping performance. It's not unusual for a twin powered sportfisherman to carry four batteries for primary use, rigged to switch-over, and another two to run a portable live-well.

thermore, there are certain species that simply respond more favorably to live bait.

Most quality boats with a reputation for salt water fishing have adequate live wells; those with larger capacities and circular designs are best. Live wells with "edges" that impede swimming capabilities injure and kill bait. Check for a functional aeration system. The best set-ups have a through hull "scoop" that forces water into the well when the boat is at speed plus a pump to draw in sea water when the vessel is stationary. An overflow drain with a diameter twice as large as the pick-up assures a constant turn-over.

There are specific situations that challenge even the best factory wells; You may have to rely on a portable system whenever there's a heavy demand. There are large, round plastic wells in a variety of capacities designed specifically for live baiting, most adapting easily to a small boat.

The size of the well depends on your fishing and boat size (consider the extra weight and how it'll factor into the

boat's performance). If 10 or 15-dozen baits are needed, well between 35 and 50-gallons is ideal. A good rule of thum is to go with the largest live well the boat can accommodat If you don't crowd bait, restricting their oxygen and alterir comfortable water temperatures, they'll keep and perform their peak throughout the day.

Setting up a functional, portable live well isn't difficul One quick and painless set-up requires a powerful deep c cle battery (buy a spare or two so you won't have to tap int your boat's power bank), a bilge pump rated around 80(gallons per hour for a well with a capacity between 30 and 5(gallons, regular bilge pump fittings, alligator clips, hos clamps, a concave brass screen, a 90-degree elbow fittin and two reinforced vinyl hoses.

Plumb the well by drilling and tapping in (sealing wit silicone) a bilge pump fitting (nozzle side out) about tw inches above the bottom, with the 90-degree elbow fastene on the inside to help channel the water in a spiraling, up ward fashion. Bore another opening with a diameter at leas twice as large near the top for the second fitting (also moun ed nozzle side out), placing the concave brass screen on th inside to keep bait and scales from clogging the passage. Re member, this overflow must have a considerably larger d ameter than the intake to prevent spillage.

Secure (clamping) a hose onto the bottom intake, cor necting the bilge pump to its opposite end. The pump shoul

Serious live-baiters recognize the importance of carrying enough ammunition to satisfy their long and determined e, forts. If you're short on live well capabilities, invest in a portabl one. Here's a 40-gallon well with a pumping system that keep nearly 15 dozen baits healthy and ready to be eaten. Note th large outlet hose and how the well and portable battery are firm ly secured.

be rigged with long electrical leads and alligator clip connectors, which will connect directly to the portable battery (secured and covered to shield the elements). The larger overflow hose attaches to the top fitting. Keep both hoses, particularly the intake, long enough to reach into the surrounding waters.

A tub full of baits is maintained by placing the bilge pump overboard (in a drifting situation) where it can draw in fresh sea water. When it's time to run, place the bilge pump inside the boat's factory well (if it's serviced by a through hull "scoop"). Providing the bilge pump's not too powerful, you can replenish the portable well's water while in transit with that system. Otherwise, you'll have to cut the juice until you shut down, keeping the pump higher than the well to prevent its contents from being siphoned out. The other alternative is to place the pump into the live well to recirculate its own water.

The advantage of a low intake position is that fresh water is forced up, establishing a constant turnover. However, the back pressure drains a battery much quicker than a topside intake (mounted directly across from the outlet and angled downward nearly 90-degrees), almost requiring double the amps to penetrate this restriction. Hard core live baiters who regularly compete in multi-day tournaments plumb their wells with both high and low intakes (using a bilge plug on the opening not in use). Most will tap the bottom intake while fishing, switching to the upper fitting to conserve battery life when tied up overnight at a marina (hooking the battery to a 10-amp charger to support the functioning pump throughout the evening). Some even replace the bilge pump with a 120-volt pump that plugs directly into the dock to continue using the bottom intake during the "off" hours. The disadvantage of continuously using the upper intake is that most of the exchange may not reach the bottom of a large well, forcing bait to crowd and gasp near the surface.

A deep cycle battery is a must because it can be recharged and operated repeatedly in its full capacity. Starter type batteries, once drained and then re-charged, are often shot by the third or fourth attempt. A quality deep cycle is suitable for both starting and deep cycle service; they have the cranking amps to turn-over marine power and, in deep-cycle use, the power to support live wells, electronics, spreader lights, electric downriggers, trolling motors, etc. Always select the most powerful battery and service it properly. This means keeping it clean and immediately recharging after each use (don't let it discharge completely since its capacity may go down and limit the duration of its charge potential). If a battery is stored for a period of time, charge it every 90-days; the quality models have built in devices that indicate their state of charge for easy monitoring. Expect between six and eight hours of live well service from a fully charged deep cycle battery and in excess of 400 charges.

THE OUTBOARD ENGINE REVOLUTION:

Today's small boater never had it so good when choosing power. The strides made by outboard manufacturers over the past two decades have been enormous, resulting in products that are state of the art and ultra dependable.

Determining what size outboard best suits your needs should reflect the type of fish pursued, distances traveled,

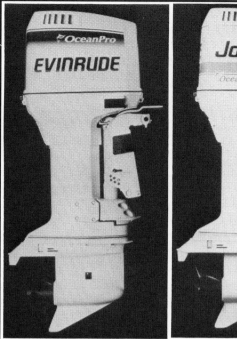
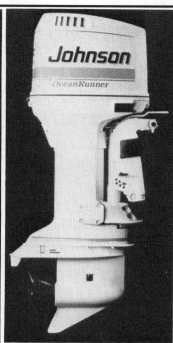

State-of-the-art outboards are more compact, lighter, stronger, more dependable and very fuel efficient. There are models available right now where even fresh water flushings and timing adjustments can be administered without firing them up! If you consistently fish many miles offshore, it's hard to beat the peace of mind of twin outboards. Furthermore, it's hard to describe the exhilaration and power one feels when the throttles are pegged.

boat size and style, fuel capacity and the desire for performance. One of the best guidelines is the maximum horsepower recommendation affixed to each boat model. For sharp performance try to select the power that's equal or close to the rating without exceeding it. All boats will run stronger with an engine surpassing that figure but foolishly overpowering can void warranties and, worse yet, insurance protection.

Don't be mislead into thinking that grossly underpowering a boat will cut gasoline consumption. It'll be an expensive mistake. For example, a 225 or 250-horsepower outboard on a fishing boat rated for a maximum of 250-horsepower will be far superior than a 140-horsepower outboard because the large block won't work nearly as hard bringing the hull up on plane. Once a cruising speed is achieved the big blocks can be throttled back to an even more conservative pace, hence saving fuel and reducing engine wear. And if a situation demands performance and top speed, they'll unleash their muscle at the drop of a throttle. The 140-horsepower mill would have to run hard to push that particular hull. The extreme load will shorten engine life, chastise performance and demand more fuel than its powerful counterparts.

Fuel efficiency is an important issue. Fortunately, most four and six cylinder outboards are loop charged, giving the angler plenty of latitude in his decision. Skiffs in the 16 through 18-foot class have the option of running a low-end horsepower V-4 outboard or a high-end horsepower three cylinder mill. The final decision often reflects how far an angler must run the skiff and if he's willing to sacrifice torque and top end speed for fuel economy. Guides who once piloted V-4 powered flats and bay skiffs are raving over their switch to three cylinder, 70 and 90-horsepower outboards. They've gained fuel economy and eliminated some transom weight, enabling them to travel farther and pole higher onto shallow flats. Keep in mind, however, that these are specialty skiffs with minimal draft and aren't dependent on triple-digit horsepower. General fishing boats of the same length, which weigh more and have sharper entries, require extra horses.

Boats between 21 and 26-feet in length are best serviced with V-6 power. Selecting the compatible horsepower will hinge on the boat's style and weight and where it'll be used. One item worth noting when dealing with outboards comparably close to each other in horsepower is that their differences generally play out at the top end. In other words, a 200 and a 225-horsepower outboard won't be that far apart in torque and mid-range performance, but the latter will excel wide open.

The debate over twin or single power on an offshore boat seems never ending, especially with the dependability and performance of modern outboards. A single outboard will slash fuel consumption almost in half and may be the better choice if you don't venture great distances offshore alone. However, it's hard to beat the peace of mind in knowing you have a "spare" should something go astray on a twin rig. Twin power should be a consideration on any boat that continually ventures out of land's sight. The extra dollars spent at the fuel pump can be rationalized as "safety insurance". Furthermore, it's hard to match the excitement of throttling up a finely tuned twin-rig, knowing that you'll be one of the first to the fish!

Performance isn't gained simply by hanging an outboard on a transom. That's where a local dealer comes in. He knows that precisely adjusting an outboard's mounting height to where its prop is just shy of cavitating (catching air) in sharp turns and following seas increases top end speed and overall efficiency. It boils down to fine tuning, encompassing the mounting height, the proper propeller and tweaking the engine for maximum performance. Experienced dealers are familiar with the right set-ups and it's best to let them handle your installations. Furthermore, selecting an outboard backed by a large dealer network assures the owner of fast and reliable service wherever he's likely to travel.

Expect the trend in high-tech outboards to produce products that are more compact, lighter, quieter, fuel efficient and responsive than past designs. There are currently some state-of-the-art V-6 outboards that, when compared to others in the same horsepower classifications, are as much as 20 and 40-pounds lighter. Think about it. On a twin installation one can shave nearly 80-pounds off the transom. There's also more emphasis on negative trim (where an outboard is trimmed under) that improves planing with stern-heavy boats or reduces the bow's attitude when trolling baits or lures in excess of eight knots, and quicker positive trim that dials in an efficient running angle. Look for modular components that make repairs a snap (a factor that can save money on labor), 35-amp alternators to handle the demands of fishing

electronics, and the ability to check an engine's timing and administer fresh water flushings without having to start it. They're out there!

THE SPORTY LOOK:

The popularity of the T-top can be traced to stylish lines, the impressive "full" look they lend a boat and their protection against harsh sunlight. Selecting one is not unlike rigging your boat. There's the need to consider your style of fishing and the relationship to the top, choosing beneficial options and determining whether your top-side arrangement will actually enhance or diminish the boat's effectiveness.

Pay attention to aerodynamics. With the speed of today's small boats it's only logical to opt for a top that's going to cut through the air with the least amount of resistance. Designs that are streamlined almost always outperform those with rounded or folded edges, which tend to trap air. Tops designed for speed and fuel efficiency resemble a spoiler or wing that is mounted level with the boat's console. In some instances a top's leading edge will be offset slightly downward to further enhance air flow. The result is an insignificant reduction in top-end speed and even less of a dent in fuel economy.

T-top fabricators usually have their own theories on best design and construction, although almost all base theirs on schedule-40 aluminum tubing and three types of covers. Acrylon fabric has been the mainstay of T-tops and is the same material used in quality boat covers. They come in a variety of bright colors so you can coordinate a particular color scheme.

Acrylon "breathes" and therefore resists mildew, but must be properly treated with Scotch Guard to prevent leaking. Weblon is a much tighter material and is impervious to leaks, although it doesn't breathe and can be subject to mildew. Both materials have a life expectancy of about five years. The third type of cover, fiberglass, may be the "look" of the future since it's durable and needs little maintenance.

A major metal fabricator on Florida's west coast has designed such a trendy, durable and functional weather shield that weighs a mere 70 pounds, only 20 pounds heavier than their fabric models. The T-top's outer finish is white gelcoat over fiberglass, with a neatly trimmed vinyl underliner to

eliminate vibration and noise. The white fiberglass top guarantees minimal heat absorption and can last indefinitely.

If you're used to carrying an assortment of console-racked rods, a T-top can be modified with rod slots on both sides. The rods slide in and out without any hitches, their tips sticking above the top. A T-top actually complements a center console by absorbing equipment that ordinarily would be fastened to the gunwales like outriggers and antennas, the latter benefitting from the extra height. Rod holders (es-

pecially if the craft is short on space), navigational lights eliminating glare and 12-volt Halogen lights directed at the cockpit for night fishing are all worthwhile advantages of a T-top. An optional electronics box will allow you to load your boat with communication and navigational gear, regardless of what console space dictates. The latest designs feature flush panels for an attractive display while hiding wiring and fuse panels. Weather protection is enhanced with adjustable, clear shields.

BOATING BASICS

PROPERLY PROPPING

The importance of the prop should be evident, since it's the final link in the transmission of power from the powerhead to the propshaft. Without it, there would be no propulsion. Any prop will propel the boat, but the "right" one will yield optimum performance.

What does a propeller really do? Essentially, the prop throws the water to the rear, causing the boat to move forward. How the prop performs is determined by how much its design affects the water with each revolution. A prop's performance capability is determined by its diameter, pitch and number of blades (most recreational props are three-bladed).

The diameter, a factor you needn't have to worry over, is engineered for each pitch, load and speed application. A high pitch prop has a small diameter and a low pitch prop has a large diameter. Other factors affecting the application are rake angle, blade shape and type of propeller.

Thru-hub exhaust is now the most widely used application, but there are some propellers which have over-the-hub exhaust. The latter is generally used on high performance craft, where getting on plane fast is not the criteria. These propellers ventilate considerably and are difficult to plane off on stern heavy boats. Cleaver designed propellers give transom lift, whereas high rake props promote bow lift.

The prop's pitch is really the amount of "twist" in the blades. The measurement of pitch is, in theory, the distance the prop will move forward in water in one revolution. A 17-inch prop theoretically moves forward 17-inches in one revolution. This is theoretical because slippage and friction work to reduce the forward movement somewhat less than 17-inches. To dial-in engine rpm by changing the prop, remember this: to increase engine rpm, a lower pitched prop should be used. Conversely, to lower engine rpm, a higher pitched prop should be used. Why is this? Using the above example, we already know that a 17-inch prop will move the boat ahead approximately 17-inches in one revolution. If we want to increase engine rpm we would select a lower pitch, let's say of 15-inches. In the same distance traveled by the 17-inch prop in one revolution (approximately 17-inches), the 15-inch prop would turn one revolution plus part of another revolution. In other words, rpm would be increased because the 15-inch prop doesn't travel as far in one revolution. A high pitched (19-inch) prop would not complete one revolution within the distance traveled by a 17-inch prop, therefore engine rpm would be reduced (i.e. fewer turns per distance traveled). You can generally expect from 150 to 200

rpm change per one-inch in pitch, provided the diameter remains the same.

Another factor to consider is whether or not the prop blades are cupped. A cupped blade is one where the trailing edge of each blade is actually cupped or "curled" up from the face of the blade. A double cupped prop simply means more cup or curl has been added to each blade on the trailing edge. Cupped props are more effective than uncupped props because they are more tolerant of turbulent water (water with high air mixture). Since this is true, cupped props can be trimmed out further without ventilating. Trimming out lifts the bow which generally raises the speed. A cupped prop also allows the engine to run higher on the transom for less gearcase drag and higher speed. The improved performance of a cupped prop leads to a "rule of thumb" which you should consider when making a prop selection. Adding cup to a prop is the equivalent of adding about 1-inch of pitch when compared to an uncupped prop of the same pitch. For example, if you replace an uncupped 17-inch aluminum prop with a double cupped 17-inch Stainless Steel prop, you'll have to remember that the latter will run at a rpm range about the same as an 18-inch uncupped prop. This, in some instances, may require that a lower pitched cupped prop be used as a replacement.

To prop a boat you need only four items:
- A selection of props
- Driver
- Tachometer
- Speedometer

Concisely stated: To determine the "best" prop, operate the boat with a driver only and prop the engine so that it operates in the upper portion of the rpm range without exceeding it. If an engine's operating range is between 5,000 and 6,000 rpm, you should use a prop that will allow the engine to turn as close to 6,000 rpm as possible. Often, as in this example, the engine will be propped with the lightest load so the engine is running near the top of its operating range. As load is added to the boat, its maximum rpm range will come down slightly, yet stay within its safe, peak zone.

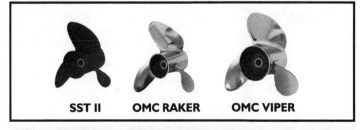

SST II   **OMC RAKER**   **OMC VIPER**

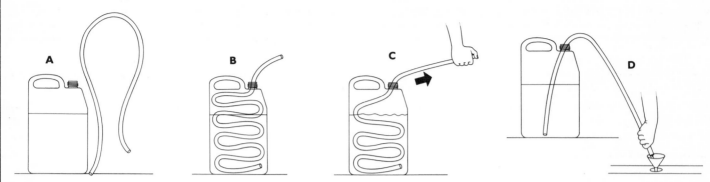

HOW TO SIPHON FUEL: Take a hose that's three times as long as the height of the gasoline container (A). Insert about three quarters of the hose into the fuel container, keeping your thumb off the opening so it'll purge air (B). Cover the hose opening with your thumb and quickly pull most of it back out in one straight movement (C). Providing your fuel supply is higher than where it's headed, getting the flow going should be no problem (D).

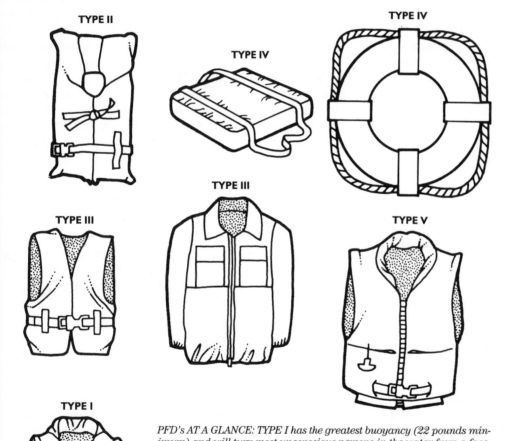

PFD's AT A GLANCE: TYPE I has the greatest buoyancy (22 pounds minimum) and will turn most unconscious persons in the water from a face-down position to one that's vertical and slightly backward. It's designed for extended survival in rough open water and where there will likely be a delay in rescue. TYPE II is sized to be put on easily and can turn an unconscious person to a vertical and slightly backward position. TYPE III is a vest-like jacket that's really a floatation aid. Both TYPE II and TYPE III are nearshore vests limited to heavily populated bays or sounds where odds are favorable for an early rescue. Both types carry about 15.5 pounds of buoyancy. TYPE IV constitutes throwable devices such as boat cushions and ring buoys. They're not designed for wear, but rather to be grasped by the user in a man overboard situation. At least one TYPE IV device has to be aboard every vessel 16 feet and over. It's the law. TYPE V is for special purposes (mostly commercial) and includes work vests, deck suits and inflatable hybrids. They contain about 17 pounds of buoyancy.

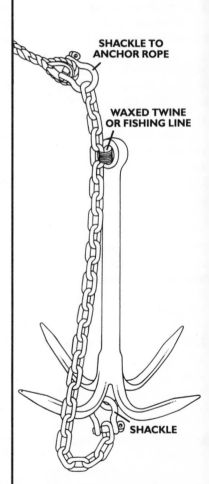

BREAKAWAY ANCHOR

Using a grapnel anchor in rocky bottom or near wrecks? Try rigging it breakaway style by attaching the shackle at the business end of the chain to its underside, using waxed twine or fishing line to secure a chain link to the anchor's shank eye. By doing so, you'll have the ability to use the boat's power to break the line and pull the anchor off backwards – if it becomes fouled. The same technique also works well with fluke-style anchors.

ook around and you'll see it everywhere. On ocean and estuary, mismatched tackle saps the effectiveness of too many anglers. Some items ooze the hand-me-down, antique appearance of another era, but the majority of rods and reels boast a newness that translates into poor selection.

Tackle is as critical as technique. A skilled fish handler finds himself seriously handicapped if he must struggle against the rod and reel instead of his quarry. A car with wheels of four different sizes may eventually get there, but the ride won't be much fun.

Every time you purchase tackle, make it part of a master plan. Focus on creating systems so that rod, reel, and line perform as a team instead of individual players. Since you can't assemble a single, universal outfit, all tackle becomes a compromise. The key lies in putting together combinations that will handle a multitude of assignments effectively.

THINK BACKWARDS

Most fishermen buy a rod and reel, adding the line after the purchase has been made. If you intend to match components for maximum performance, think backwards. Start with the breaking strength of the line you intend to use. In making that decision, you'll want to consider the species you seek, your own skill as an angler, personal preference (heavy or light), and the habitat of your quarry. Wrestling some unseen denizen out of a rock-strewn lair or snaking an oversized critter from an orchard of pilings dictates stronger line. To enjoy the long, reel-screaming runs of a shallow water speedster, opt for light line and corresponding tackle.

If you insist on fishing larger diameter line on a small reel and whippy rod, you inadvertently sabotage the design of the system. Light line on a rod engineered to lift a small sedan off the bottom doesn't make sense. Pick the line first and then find a rod engineered for that breaking strength. When you add a reel of the appropriate size, you have a com-

bination tailored to take on anything that picks up the bait or smashes a lure.

Assembling a matching outfit for offshore trolling doesn't pose much of a problem. Rods and reels are already designated by the line they are designed to handle. This is called class tackle. You simply spool 30-pound test line on a 30-pound reel and attach it to a 30-pound rod. These classes match the record-keeping classifications of the International Game Fish Association (IGFA).

It's not that simple with casting and non-class tackle. Those who label rods insist on recommending too wide a range of line sizes. You'll make a better choice if you consider the lower limits rather than the higher ones. If the label tells you the rod can handle 8-pound to 20-pound test line, for example, consider the optimum to be 8-pound or 10-pound test. A properly designed rod performs best within a relatively narrow range.

CHOOSING A ROD

The right rod for any situation must be able to present the bait or lure effortlessly, set the hook with authority, do battle effectively, and perform well with the breaking strength of the line you intend to use. Every rod is a compromise. Start

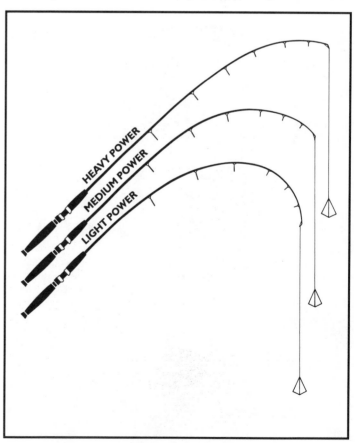

It takes more force to bend the tip of a heavy power rod, whereas a softer tip offers less power (illustrated here). Action refers to a rod's taper, to the spot on the blank where it flexes. A fast-action rod, for example, flexes within the top quarter or third of the blank, while a moderate action develops half-way to two-thirds down the blank.

Selecting offshore trolling outfits doesn't pose much of a problem because rods and reels are already designated by the line they are designed to handle.

the selection process by analyzing your needs objectively. If you envision yourself slugging it out with trophy-size critters, focus on the fish-fighting characteristics. You may have to sacrifice a little on presentation, but the tradeoff could be important. When it is more important to get a bait or lure to the fish than doing battle, the fighting qualities of the stick become secondary.

Picking a quality rod starts with the material from which the blank is made. Graphite has become the material of choice, but it is considerably more expensive than fiberglass. The newer or second generation fiberglass (called S-glass) performs remarkably well and rates as a worthwhile compromise. The original fiberglass is known as E-glass. S-glass weighs less and is exceptionally strong.

All graphite is not the same. Right now, you'll find at least three generations of graphite available with at least two more generations waiting in the wings for their debut. The key, however, lies in how well a blank has been engineered. Perhaps the best advice suggests that you place your confidence in a reputable manufacturer and a knowledgeable dealer.

Modulus of elasticity or simply modulus refers to the stiffness of the material or its resistance to deflection. The stiffer the material, the more sensitive it is to vibrations. With a higher modulus, you can feel a strike more easily and often cast with less effort. Unless you actually cast a graphite rod or test its lifting power, it's difficult to determine performance. Waving it around a store like a cavalry saber proves counterproductive and tells you nothing.

A properly designed rod performs best within a relatively narrow range. If the label tells you the rod can handle 8-pound to 20-pound-test line, consider the optimum to be near the lower fringes.

Let's dispel the fallacy of a whippy rod. Too many fishermen erroneously believe that soft, whippy rods make casting a dream (particularly with light lines) and tire a fish quickly. Floppy tips do little more than telegraph a less than desireable design. Monofilament line provides all the cushion you need even with very light lines. It stretches at least 25 percent under load and that makes the outfit extremely forgiving.

You should check a rod's action, which represents the taper of the blank. Hold the butt of the rod at your belt buckle and sweep it back and forth parallel to the floor. Look down the shaft and determine where it is flexing. If the flex takes place near the tip, it's a fast action rod. Blanks that flex about half-way down constitute medium action, while those that flex just beyond the foregrip are slow action.

Power translates into a blank's stiffness. The same taper is often available in several degrees of stiffness. To fight fish effectively, you must have adequate reserve power in a rod. When you apply a load, the strain travels down the blank toward the butt. A soft tip contributes nothing to absorbing the load. The muscle in a rod lies near the butt. That's where the reserve lifting power takes over, enabling you to pressure a fish. If that power isn't there, it's going to be a long frustrating battle.

The number of guides on a rod offer a clue to construction quality. Whether you are shopping for a spinning stick or a conventional rod, make sure it has at least five guides plus a tiptop. Anything less and you know the manufacturer is trying to reduce his costs. Guides lead the line along the curvature of the blank, eliminating any sharp radii. To test a rod, rig it up with line and pull. The line should scribe an arc that follows the blank. If it doesn't, look for another model.

The best length for most saltwater assignments center around 7 feet. Shorter rods seldom cast as well and those over 7-1/2 feet pose problems. Surf rods stand out as an exception, of course, with the jetty models around 8-feet and those tailored for work on the sand measuring 11 to 13 feet.

If you can find rods with short butts (assuming they meet the other criteria), consider them seriously. Rod makers produce products with longer butts because they appear more formidable and they sell. To the unknowing customer, the short butt looks like a design mistake. In fighting a fish, a shorter butt puts the reel closer to your body. That enables you to lock your arms against your side and use your body. Reaching forward for a reel handle fatigues arms, shoulders and back.

Offshore enthusiasts have a choice between stand-up tackle and regulation trolling gear. The longer, regulation rods prove superior when you sit in a fighting chair and do battle. If you plan to belly up to the covering board and remain on your feet, try the stand-up rod. Stand-ups have more guides than regulation rods and a special taper to facilitate pumping. Models with roller guides seem to be a better choice than rods with standard, fixed foot guides.

At one time, serious anglers believed that only one-piece rods delivered maximum performance. In those days, ferruling created dead spots. The notion lingers in some quarters. If you were blindfolded, you could not tell the difference between many of the one-piece and two-piece rods today. Four-piece rods are becoming increasingly common for travelling anglers and they, too, boast excellent ferruling.

ADD THE RIGHT REEL

The reel forms the third leg of the tackle triangle and must be targeted for both the line and the rod you plan to use. Too large or too small a reel destroys the system concept, becoming a burden instead of an asset. An impressive number of reels in a multitude of sizes crowds the marketplace, making the ultimate selection somewhat difficult.

The starting point centers on two primary features: adequate line capacity for the breaking strength of the line and a smooth drag. Once you have cleared those essential hurdles, you can focus on the features. This approach applies equally to any type of reel.

For smaller species, think in terms of 150 to 200 yards of line as a minimum. With some bait casting models, capacity may be less than that, forcing a compromise. You can live with less line on a bait caster if the fish you catch are not noted for sustained runs. Huskier critters require 200 to 300 yards of line (and sometimes more). Trolling reels tailored for offshore waters should be spooled with a minimum of 350 to 500 yards of line.

Surviving a sustained run is only one facet of line capacity. The diameter of line on the spool determines the actual length of line you will recover with each revolution of the reel handle. That's why you want the spool at least half full, even after that long run. Think about this before plunking cash or credit card on the counter and walking off with a reel that fails to do the job.

A good drag releases line smoothly at precisely the preset pressure without any increase or decrease. The more drag surface in a reel coupled with washers from quality material serve as an indication of a smooth drag. Multi-stage drags add more surface area in a limited space.

Check the range of adjustments by turning the lever from free spool to full drag. You don't want a drag that remains loose through the tightening process until the very end and then locks suddenly. The rod tip mirrors drag performance on the water. When a fish takes line, the tip should drop and remain relatively stationary. If the tip jumps up and down, the drag is erratic.

A lever drag reel such as one might fish for big game must have a full-functioning free spool regardless of the amount of preset drag on the reel. Some models fail this test, handicapping the angler who must drop back to a fish without resistance. Any tension, pressure, or binding transmits a signal to the fish that something is wrong and it may drop the bait.

How many features you want on a reel beyond these basics becomes a matter of budget and personal choice. Do check the gear ratio between the pinion and the drive gear. It's expressed as 4:1, 5:1, and so forth. That means that the

Spinning reels intended for small species should carry at least 150 yards of line. Maintaining a full spool promotes maximum casting distances.

Some trolling reels offer two speed capabilities and increased line capacities. It may pay to go that route if you're chasing the big ones. This angler was glad he did because a 700-pound-class blue marlin dumped 3/4 of the spool (nearly straight down!) before he was able to regain line. The fish was boated three hours later.

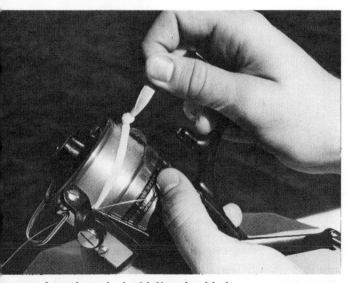

Spare reel spools packed with line should always accompany an angler, especially when traveling to foreign waters. You can pop a fresh line in seconds.

11

spool turns so many times when the handle makes one revolution. The higher the ratio, the faster the spool turns and the more line you can recover with each full spin of the handle. In the tradeoff, you lose power. Put a load on the line and it becomes difficult to turn the handle with a high gear ratio.

Some reels now offer two speeds with the ability to shift during the battle. You can use the speed gearing during the retrieve or to take in line quickly, down-shifting to the power gear when you have to pump your quarry. Analyze the type of fishing you will do and then decide on an equitable compromise.

Magnetic casting control in bait casting reels have reduced the need for an educated thumb. You can adjust the control to match your skill. The more dampening you dial in, the shorter your casts will be. Some of the latest entries are as sleek as sports cars and perform about as well.

Most folks encounter problems in deciding on which spinning reel to buy. The guidelines listed above apply first. Then, check the the bail and the roller. The roller should still turn under pressure and you certainly want a bail that you can close manually in addition to its automatic feature.

The majority of new reels enable the user to switch from right to left hand retrieve by changing the handle assembly from one side to the other. If you're considering a reel with a rear drag, be aware that the drag washers must be squeezed in a small space. Front drag models almost always incorporate a better drag system.

Regardless of how large a spinning reel may be, 20-pound test line is about the maximum you can cast effectively. You'll find anglers who insist on spooling heavier line, but they have knowingly or unknowingly exceeded the limits. At the other end of the spectrum, if the spool on a spinning reel is 2 inches or less, you should not use line heavier than 10-pound test. Finally, stick with open-faced spinning rather than spin casting or closed-faced.

The more expensive offshore trolling reels reflect the breaking strength of the line they are intended to handle. They'll be labelled as 30-pound, 50-pound, and so forth. Major manufacturers offer both standard and wide models in the different sizes and some reels boast the two-speed feature. Unfortunately, the day hasn't come when spinning reels will be designated 6 pound, 10 pound, 12 pound, etc., but we'll keep campaigning.

Less expensive reels in this category still follow the "0" system (4/0, 6/0, 9/0, etc.). A 4/0 reel takes 30-pound test line, a 6/0 matches 50-pound, and a 9/0 proves ideal for 80-pound. Usually, these reels have star wheels to adjust the drag rather than levers.

THE TRAVELING ANGLER

Anglers seem to be plagued with the decision of whether or not to take tackle when they travel to other fishing destinations and plan to charter a boat or hire a guide. No one appreciates the inconvenience more than outdoor journalists when it comes to lugging rod cases through airports or struggling with extra baggage. To us, having quality tackle on hand that includes full spools of fresh line is the cheapest insurance you can buy for a successful trip.

The same gear you prefer back home usually works well on other waters, providing the species you seek are the same relative size. If you deal with featherweight gear at home an plan to do battle with some ornery critter that eats anythin it wants, you might have to rely on someone else's tackl

When your destination is outside the United States, tak your own tackle regardless of what the lodge owner recom mends. It is difficult and expensive to obtain and maintai quality tackle in other countries and particularly in remote l cations. Spooling fresh line before a reel is half-full ranks a a luxury rather than an essential. Mismatched combination often encompass the rule rather than the exception.

Within the continental United States, you may have choice. Guides who specialize in a specific type of fishin and particularly light tackle often have excellent equipmen on board. If you were going to fish the flats in the Florid Keys, for example, you can count on the leading guides t have the right tackle for the task and it's in excellent shap When you make the booking, you should be able to ascertai whether or not your own gear will be necessary.

Put to sea aboard an offshore charter boat with a targe market of tourists who walk down the dock and you'll wis you had your own rods and reels. You can count on the lin to be particularly heavy, so if you want to fish lighter monofi ament you'll have to bring your own. These boats cater to th casual angler who probably doesn't know whether the tack le is good or bad. That should tell you all you need to kno

If you do pack your own outfits, take more tackle tha you expect to use, especially if you are going to be in an are where the nearest tackle shop is a plane ride away. We think i terms of three. In deciding what to carry, we'll settle on the pr mary class of equipment. You'll always find us with at least on outfit heavier than the norm and another that is much lighte

The three outfit spread is relative. If the basic situatio dictates 12-pound test, the lighter outfit would probably b 8-pound and the heavier one about 17-pound or even 2(pound test. A 30-pound offshore outfit can be supported wit 12 or 20-pound on the light side and 50-pound or 80-poun on the heavy side. Invariably, an oversized denizen will suc denly show and you'll be glad you had the huskier tackle. the fish prove to be finicky feeders, switch to the lighter lin Even when fishing in home waters, the three outfit approac makes sense.

Travelling sports lack confidence in the old-standby lure they use at home, figuring that fish-catching, local favorite are the only thing to use at the final destination. No matte where you fish in the world, most of the lures from you home waters will produce results provided you are skilled i fishing them.

Whenever you take to the road or the airlanes, pack a assortment of leadheaded jigs. They'll cover a multitude of as signments. Add some topwater plugs that make noise an even a few darter-types. Pack a handful of swimming plug and perhaps a few that sink and can be counted down. Tha should get you through most casting situations anywher you choose to fish.

Finally, stuff an adequate supply of confidence into you bags and rod cases. It will help convince you that your tack le will work well and your lure selection is perfect for th task. And if your going out of the country, don't overloo packing hooks, leader material, sinkers, and other termina gear. You may be glad you did.

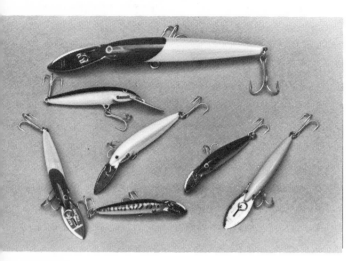

...wimming lures come in all sizes. These deep divers can be ...caled to the size of the species they're intended for and either ...ast or trolled. Whereas inshore fish such as speckled trout will ...eadily consume a small plug, it usually takes the action and vi-...ration of the larger ones to toll in the offshore warriors.

...rtificial lures are a sure-fix for the salt water angler. That ...ay be a bold statement unless you've considered that they ...ork equally well both inshore and offshore and come in all ...orms, sizes and colors. There are versatile models that pro-...uce on a variety of gamefish over a wide range of situations ...nd then there are those tailored to specific species and feed-...g environments.

Lure applications vary among anglers. Some enthusiasts ...sh nothing but artificials, firmly believing that there's a cer-...ain level of prestige that goes with fooling fish on one, while ...thers classify them as specialty baits which excel under cer-...ain conditions. Regardless of the scenario, the incorporating ...ngler doesn't leave the dock without an array of lures ap-...licable to his waters.

There are numerous considerations involved in selecting

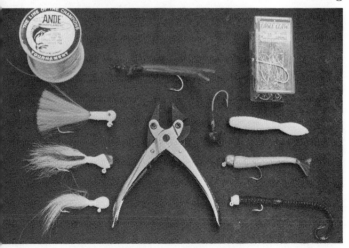

...asting artificials come in all shapes and sizes. Sometimes it's ...rd to avoid metallic leaders, but rigging one with monofila-...ent is the surest way to fast action.

the most productive lure for the task at hand and there are always exceptions to the rule. However, some of the best lure technicians stick to a few basic guidelines encompassing size, shape, color and rigging. By closely matching a lure to the local forage, it only stands to reason that you'll draw more strikes. This is especially evident in feeding frenzies on an abundance of a specific bait where gamefish can become very selective.

Retrievals also play a big part. Pay attention to where and how baitfish are moving. Try and mimic their actions with a top water plug if they're milling at the surface. If they're marked on a recorder huddling deep, a sinking/diving plug or leadhead may be the answer. Always begin by fishing the edges (including the area above and below submerged pods), making the lure stand out as an injured or distressed baitfish; These are the ones often singled out as an easy meal. Sometimes it takes a wild, erratic retrieve to entice a fish, perhaps by a lure differing sharply from the original choice. Experimentation is the key. If the typical "fish catchers" are having an off day, try sending in the "second string" and vary-ing their actions.

Some of the most consistent catches come from lures at-tached directly to the fishing line or a very light leader. Choos-ing the lightest leader that still offers adequate protection improves a lure's running capabilities and is less noticeable by fish. There are occasions, however, where heavy monofil-ament or wire leaders can't be avoided. Adhere to the same principle and try not to over-gun the system.

Another key in getting the most from plugs, spoons and jigs is to join leader and lure with a "loop" connection, en-abling them to swim freely around the circumference; snug-ging down a leader will inhibit a lure's performance unless it's equipped with an eye-ring.

SWIMMING PLUGS FOR TROLLING:

Balsa wood or hard plastic swimming plugs depict nat-ural baits more closely than most other forms of artificials. They're readily available, competitively priced and a cinch to rig and fish. In addition to casting, swimming plugs trolled through estuaries, channel edges, inlets or passes, along beaches and rips produce a number of key species including trout, bluefish, striped bass, tarpon and snook.

One of their newest frontiers is offshore. Gulf coast an-glers trolling diving plugs around oil platforms find them dev-astating on wahoo, kings, bonito and tuna, while southern U.S. and Bahamas anglers plying the reefs are taking kingfish, wahoo and dolphin on top and grouper, amberjack and snap-per off the bottom. A pelagic that seems custom made for a swimming plug, however, is the yellowfin tuna. A technique recently perfected off the coast of Louisiana mixes several diving plugs with small trolling artificials. The impact the plugs are making on yellowfins, many exceeding 100-pounds, are astounding. It's a matter of time before word spreads throughout the entire offshore community.

Offshore trollers have three basic models to choose from:

Swimming plugs have evolved into a deadly offshore tool. Wahoo (pictured here) find their action irresistible and tuna can't live without them.

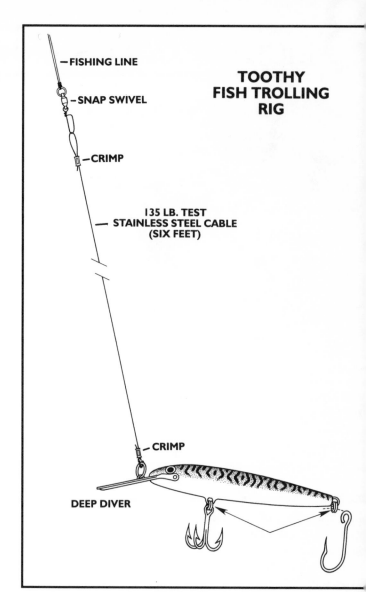

TOOTHY FISH TROLLING RIG

— FISHING LINE

— SNAP SWIVEL

— CRIMP

135 LB. TEST STAINLESS STEEL CABLE (SIX FEET)

— CRIMP

DEEP DIVER

wobbling plugs (weighted, lipless designs for erratic action), floating/diving (short lips and minimal weight) and sinking/deep running (internal weights and elongated lips). As mentioned earlier, consider the local baitfish and try to size your plugs accordingly. Whereas school kings, mackerel, bonito and bluefish have no qualms over nailing plugs in the six-inch range, they may be intimidated or even hard to hook by larger versions. Yellowfins, wahoo, dolphin and smoker kings respond favorably to plugs in the 10-inch range. Matching the natural baitfish colors is a pretty safe route to success, even though brighter shades and fluorescent score frequently. Some captains swear by using light colors on bright days and dark hues under overcast conditions and on downriggers, believing the darker shades permeate farther through the water. One thought worth remembering is that trolled plugs emit a pulsating vibration fish can sense, a big advantage in cloudy or roiled water.

A simple, yet proven offshore pattern consists of four deep divers on flat lines fished directly behind the boat, and a fifth one on a downrigger or planer. The closest bait should ride where the prop wash fades, staggering the others about 30 feet apart (it's not necessary to fish baits far back because of the slower trolling speeds, around five knots). Most plugs seem to have their own tracking characteristics, even though they can be tuned at the lip. Watch how they track and then, if necessary, rearrange the rods to design the best spread.

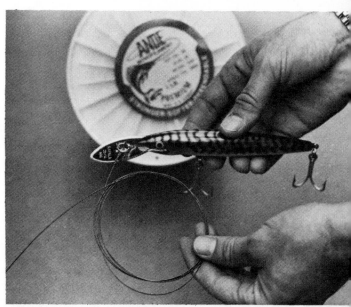

When dealing with toothy offshore species, use a stainless steel cable testing at approximately 135 pounds. The thin diameter creates less drag and the material's flexibility guards it against kinks and breaks. Replacing the trebles with a durable single hook makes it a snap to free a lure from a fish's jaw.

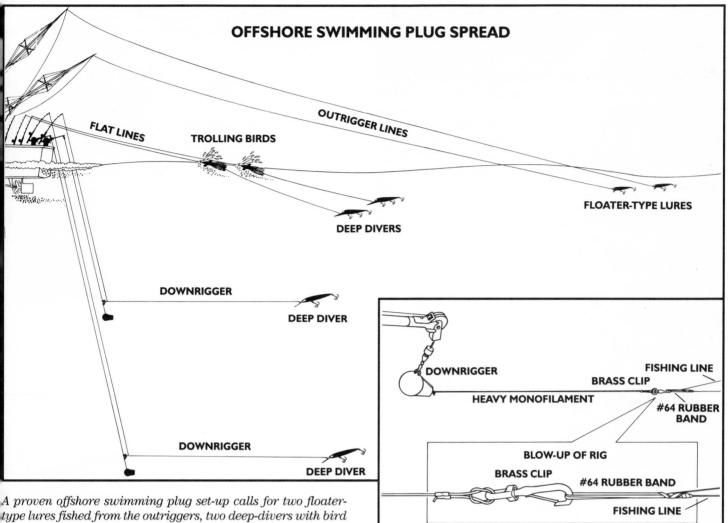

OFFSHORE SWIMMING PLUG SPREAD

FLAT LINES

OUTRIGGER LINES

TROLLING BIRDS

FLOATER-TYPE LURES

DEEP DIVERS

DOWNRIGGER

DEEP DIVER

DOWNRIGGER

DEEP DIVER

DOWNRIGGER

HEAVY MONOFILAMENT

FISHING LINE

BRASS CLIP

#64 RUBBER BAND

BLOW-UP OF RIG

BRASS CLIP

#64 RUBBER BAND

FISHING LINE

A proven offshore swimming plug set-up calls for two floater-type lures fished from the outriggers, two deep-divers with bird attractors on the flat lines and two deep-divers staggered in the depths on downriggers.

An effective spread is one that covers a major portion of the water column. Such a design may include six lines: two deep divers on downriggers staggered in the depths, two floater/divers fished off the outriggers and two deep divers on the flat lines, each following a trolling bird (which adds extra commotion that may draw in a fish). Lures on the outriggers require a tight setting on the release clips or tag lines with Number 64 rubber bands; enough resistance is needed to imbed the hooks before the line and clip(s) part. The same strength rubber band can also secure the fishing line to a locked downrigger clip. Remember to pay out each lure slowly to keep them from doubling back onto their leader.

Leader material varies with species. Whereas monofilament is best on fish such as bonito, striped bass, snook and tarpon, the acute dentition of the likes of kings and wahoo demand more protection. Stainless steel cable is a popular offshore leader material because its thin diameter creates less drag than a heavy monofilament. Furthermore, its flexibility guards it against the kinks and breaks that haunt wire leader. Take about six-feet of 135-pound test leader and with the appropriate sleeves form two "loops", one that the lure can swim on and the other to latch onto the fishing line's snap swivel.

Stock hooks should withstand the pressure of tackle approaching 20-pound test, but an upgrade to extra-strength

Because swimming plugs need a firm drag setting to drive the hooks into a striking fish, outrigger and downrigger clips must be adjusted accordingly. One trick that works on a downrigger is to attach a short length of heavy monofilament to the weight. Crimp or tie a brass clip onto the opposite end. After the lure is paid out, wrap a number 64 rubber band on the fishing line and then attach the rubber band to the clip. When a fish strikes, the tension produced before the rubber band snaps usually results in a solid hook set.

trebles or a durable single hook (recommended for catch and release fishing) is added insurance on heavier gear. Experts on offshore swimming plugs subscribe to a specialized fighting style, primarily to prevent straightening or breaking hooks. Other than large tunas (or the occasional marlin) where 30 and 50-pound test tackle and extra-strength hooks are mandatory, most offshore fish can be subdued on stout spinning outfits and live bait tackle loaded with 300-yards of 20 or 25-pound test line and stock hooks. Drags are set no heavier than four pounds on both line classes, forcing a fish to wear itself down by running hard and long (similar to the live bait/small treble hooks kingfish technique applied off the Carolinas and northern Florida). Once it settles (chasing if necessary to retain a safe amount of line), play the fish with slow, smooth pumps, tempering instincts to apply additional pressure. Lead the fish to the gaff with the rod rather than try and handle the leader (hence the short length) and be aware of any last-second surges. You'll be amazed at how quickly a fish will spend itself when subdued in this fashion.

THE MANY MOODS OF THE LEADHEADS:

The leadhead (jig) is unquestionably the most important and versatile lure any angler can carry. Comprised of molten lead, a hook, a shot of enamel paint and some form of skirting (usually nylon), they can penetrate and catch fish anywhere in the water column. Furthermore, their compact size, enabling fish to inhale them in one shot, heightens hook-up percentages. Compared to most plugs, spoons and offshore lures that have an inherent action, the leadhead's rhythm is controlled largely by the angler.

There are designs favoring certain situations that anglers should be aware of. For instance, those with flat or compressed sides, often called lima-beans, have fluttering instincts mimicking an injured baitfish when hopped up or free-spooled through a water column. Their wide bodies catch more water than the streamlined, arrow designs, giving them a slower, more erratic path. When a quick, precise retrieve is needed, the arrow-tapered jigs are best. Often the choice of deep jiggers who also concentrate on the mid and upper water columns, the arrow head tracks straight and is easily ambushed by pelagics such as bonito, kingfish, mackerel, wahoo, dolphin, tuna and barracuda. There's a specialty jig that's hopped or snaked across grass beds and flats. It's weighted so that its flat side (concealing the hook) rides upright, posing little threat of a snag. It's a favorite for redfish, bonefish, muttons, permit and other "rooters".

The leadhead jig ranks as the most versatile lure any angler can carry. It's just as effective snaked through the mid and upper water column as it is bouncing bottom. The trick lies in penetrating the depths with the least amount of weight and with the lightest feasible leader system. Tipping with bait doubles its effectiveness.

VARIATIONS OF A THEME

The plastic grub is also a killer on the flats and estuarie A curled tail grub of about four inches can be retrieved stead

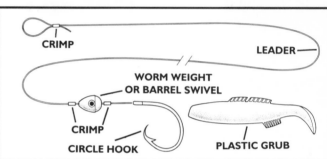

A plastic curled tail grub shows no mercy on flats and estuar residents, plus it's easy to make. It can be rigged weedless an snaked through grasses and flats, or with a circle hook and heavier weight for bouncing inlets and beaches for tarpon.

ly, relying on its pulsating tail to draw attention, or hoppe across flats and grass beds where its tail rides enticing above the bottom. The lure is rigged in a weedless fashion b reversing the hook point back into the body. A small spl shot or worm weight, slid down the leader and fastened i front of the grub to prevent slippage, enables it to be ca critical distances, and to sink. Of course, they're also availab with their own leadheads for general fishing application

Plastic grubs come in a multitude of colors but lead heads are limited mainly to white, yellow and pink. Som colors work better for certain species and choosing the be one may take some experimenting. One solution is for two a glers to fish contrasting colors in a similar manner. If one co or excels, switch over. Probably the best advice in choosin a jig is to go with the lightest one that will get the job don Inshore anglers jigging channels and pot holes need them t be heavy enough to reach their target yet small enough to b consumed, whereas offshore jiggers penetrating conside able depths need a weight to overpower a current.

The lightest tackle and leaders for your type of fishin also improve a jig's action by allowing it to sink more efficient compared to the resistance generated by the expanded d ameters of heavier monofilament. Using a loop knot gives th jig extra latitude. Monofilament leaders are less visible tha wire, but sometimes a metallic trace is necessary on toot fish. Try tying in a few inches of a light wire to a monofilament leader via an Albright Special. The wire should guard against a cut-off and the predominately mono leader will still preserve a jig's action. With species such as mackerel and bluefish, substituting the wire trace with a heavy monofilament (connecting it to the leader with a Surgeon's knot) may draw more strikes, despite inflating the cut-off risk. Inspect the entire leader system for abrasion after each hit and fish.

Scent increases a lure's potential by adding another dimension. Tipping a jig with natural bait often doubles its effectiveness. Although "tipping" is frowned upon by jigging purists, it has saved many a day by catching fish that otherwise had been reluctant to strike plain iron. In some forms of fishing a whole bait is impaled on a jig and sent to the bottom, using the lead merely as an attractive weight.

Sound is another factor that's just beginning to surface in jig fishing. A Miramar, Florida, based distributor of a popular line of leadheads is experimenting with sound chambers (tiny ball bearings contained within a plastic sphere) on deep jigs, basing his approach on the distress signals emitted by jeopardized baitfish. If a jig snaked through a water column can incorporate a similar sound, it should have that much more appeal.

SPECIALIZED RETRIEVES

Jigging techniques are as varied as the fish they're intended for. When casting to schooling fish like mackerel and bluefish, try an ultra-fast, whipping retrieve, and one that's straight and quick for bonito and tuna. Speed enhances the fishes perception of a fleeing bait and forces them to strike recklessly out of competition. Never slow a jig's retrieve by the boat, especially if a fish is in pursuit. Pull it from the water, cast it out and retrieve it back through the school. Holding a rod high above your head and snaking a jig across the surface adds an enticing splashing sound and camouflages the hardware, a powerful technique that works when fish become wise.

Deep jiggers seeking benthic species need to concentrate on the final 10 percent of the water column. Outside of isolated cases where catches have been made at mid and upper depths, most bottom fish are reluctant to venture far from their lairs. Free-spool a jig that's heavy enough to reach bottom, engaging the drag once it hits. With short, sweeping motions, hop the jig off the bottom or just above irregular structure. Free-spool back to bottom and continue jigging until the current planes the jig out of range. Bottom fish, such as groupers and snappers, are slow to moderate swimmers but have the ability to turn abruptly on a hopping jig, rarely missing it. Most pelagics rely on blazing speed to catch food, yet lack the acute, tight quarter maneuverability of the bottom feeders. That's why it's best to tighten up on the jigging and increase the lure's speed as it's retrieved to the surface. If it's tracking in a straight line, it'll be easier for a pelagic to consume. Drop down and repeat the technique once the jig reaches the surface.

Impaling a bait like a whole ballyhoo or squid on a jig and placing it on or near the bottom is a good method for big fish. It's a "lazy" way to fish because you're only checking on the proper depth and either holding the rod or setting it in the gunwale. One angle is to deploy such a bait from a rod holder and deep jig with another outfit. As the current sweeps the baited jig off the bottom it'll become fair game for pelagics. Just retrieve the line, check the bait and send it back down about every ten minutes.

The same technique of drifting a jig works in certain inshore situations. A weedless, weighted grub that's allowed to drag over grass beds or patchy bottom, as anglers cast and retrieve other lures, has surprised many.

HARD HITTING TECHNIQUE FOR HIGH SPEED PLASTICS:

Billfish anglers who seriously pursue blue marlin have perfected their trolling lures with either a free swinging or stiff trailing hook. Opinions on the better set-up vary among captains. Proponents of the stiff-rig claim the added rigidity accounts for more solid hook-ups, while fans from the other camp believe the limber set-up doesn't hinder a lure's running capabilities (like the stiff rig) and holds much better in a fish's jaw because there's no leverage to work it free.

A new twist in lure rigging and fishing, however, is bound to revolutionize this specialized technique. Originating in the Caribbean and perfected by a few world-class captains, the system replaces the tandem rig with a large, single hook. One version connects the hook with a strand of heavy aircraft cable that's long enough to position it just inside the lure's tail (so there's no interference in setting the hook). A monofilament leader of around 400-pound test is used and it's crimped to the cable loop (which rides within a thimble or plastic tubing to prevent chafing) behind the lure's head.

The interesting concept is how they're fished. Once set into an attractive spread, reel drags are advanced only enough to hold them in place. Outrigger clips replace tag lines (which impede this system) and they're tightened only

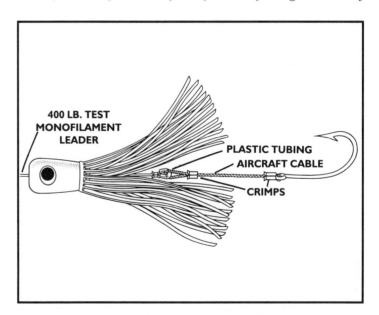

400 LB. TEST MONOFILAMENT LEADER

PLASTIC TUBING
AIRCRAFT CABLE

CRIMPS

Single hooks and drop-backs with marlin lures? You bet, and those perfecting this technique are experiencing hook-up ratios exceeding 80 percent. The hook is attached to a strand of heavy aircraft cable and rides just inside the skirt (a thimble or plastic tubing protects the monofilament leader from the cable at their connection). A light setting enables a marlin to gain complete possession of the lure, setting up a positive striking angle before the drag's fully engaged.

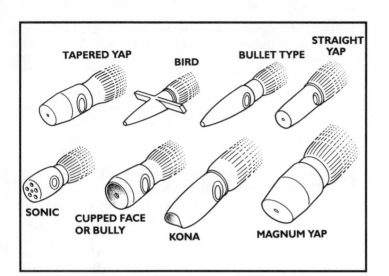

TAPERED YAP **BIRD** **BULLET TYPE** **STRAIGHT YAP**

SONIC **CUPPED FACE OR BULLY** **KONA** **MAGNUM YAP**

The many faces of the offshore trolling lure: Tapered Yap produces more a wobbling action over a wide range of trolling speeds. The Bird caus commotion as its wings beat the surface. It usually precedes a lure as a te er, but some anglers rig it for action. Bullet Type lures are engineered run just beneath the surface and at high trolling speeds. They're a favor among tuna and wahoo anglers, often deployed when running to and fre the fishing grounds. The Straight Yap is a versatile lure performing best tween seven and 10 knots. It tracks dead straight, making it an easy to get. Sonic heads are similar to straight yaps but push more air throu their vents, heightening smoking abilities. Cupped Face or Bully hea push water for their tight wobbling actions. The cupped heads genere more drag and some anglers believe this slight popping action has a m jor audible advantage. The spooned-out head of a Kona lure gives it a da ing, swimming action. It pulls well at slower speeds and is a good rough u ter lure. The Magnum design's larger diameter pushes more water. It h an action similar to the tapered yap.

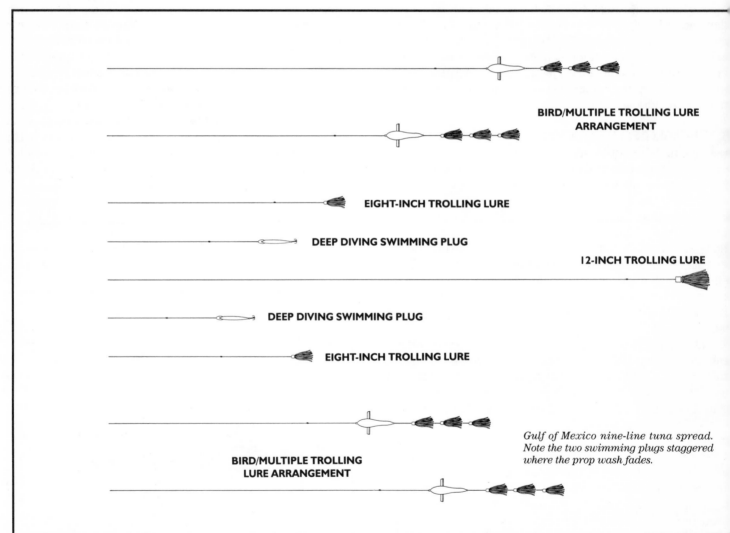

BIRD/MULTIPLE TROLLING LURE ARRANGEMENT

EIGHT-INCH TROLLING LURE

DEEP DIVING SWIMMING PLUG

12-INCH TROLLING LURE

DEEP DIVING SWIMMING PLUG

EIGHT-INCH TROLLING LURE

BIRD/MULTIPLE TROLLING LURE ARRANGEMENT

Gulf of Mexico nine-line tuna spread. Note the two swimming plugs staggered where the prop wash fades.

to withstand the rigors of a lure trudging through the sea. With as little as four pounds of drag and no "clickers", the marlin, feeling little resistance after it strikes, swims off with the lure. The angler removes the outfit from the gunwale (aiming it directly at the fish to further reduce pressure) and transfers it to the fighting chair. He then advances the drag lever to the strike setting and hits the fish. Despite the traditional belief that a fish will spit a plastic lure, a hot marlin isn't too eager to give up something that has triggered it into

striking, at least not in the time it takes to set the hook. Th method has netted hook-up percentages exceeding 80 pe cent because the fish have ample time to gain complete po session of the lure and to turn sideways or completely awa from the boat before the line comes tight, setting up a bett striking angle. The single hook also promotes conservatio and safety, since very few fish swallow the lure and there a no tandem rigs to threaten the wire man or fish after a r lease.

Catching proves to be much more fun than fishing. The transition occurs the instant you can tease or tempt a fish into striking. The exhilarating sensation of an unseen critter engulfing a bait or the unforgettable sight of an excited gamester crashing a surface offering cancels out the boredom of waiting. Adrenalin surges through the body, uniting muscle and thought. The battle is about to begin.

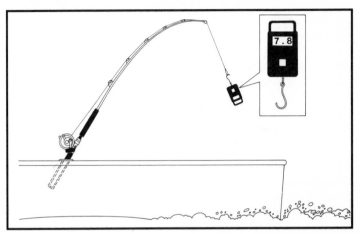

Set the strike drag with the rod in a holder. The scale should read between 25 and 33 percent of the unknotted line strength when the drag starts to slip. Thirty-pound-test line (shown here) should have a strike drag setting of between 7.5 and ten pounds.

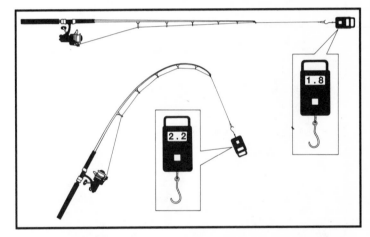

If you set the drag on a light-tackle outfit (12-pound test is illustrated here) with the rod tip pointed at the scale (top), the reading should be about 15 percent of the unknotted line strength. When the rod is in the fighting position (bottom) friction will increase the drag.

Light tackle experts live by precision drags. Challenge a hard running gamester like this kingfish with an erratic drag and you'll never get this close.

SETTING THE DRAG

Before you start fishing, the drag on the reel must be set correctly. Think of drag as a resistance to rotation rather than a brake. It challenges the fish to pull against controlled pressure without breaking the line. Too much drag or a spool that stops and fails to yield line ends the battle abruptly.

The minimum amount of drag occurs when the rod tip points directly at the fish or the spot where the line enters the water. Begin to lift the rod above the horizontal and the amount of drag increases because of the friction created by the rod blank and the guides. Understanding the mechanics of drag plays a critical role in slugging it out with any critter.

A scale doesn't have an opinion, making it the ideal tool for setting drag accurately. Rig up the rod, attach the hook or lure to the scale, point the rod directly at the scale, and move it backward until the line begins to slip. That's the reading you want. It will tell you the minimum amount of drag if you point the rod at the fish.

For lines testing 20 pounds or less, the drag should be set at roughly 15 percent of the unknotted line test, measured with the rod tip pointing at the scale. Fifteen pound test requires just over 2 pounds and 10-pound test calls for about 1-1/2 pounds of drag.

Offshore anglers and some inshore aficionados prefer to measure drag with the rod in a holder rather than pointing at the scale. The rule of thumb suggests 25 percent of the unknotted strength for lines testing up to 50 pounds and 30 percent for 80 and 130 pound line.

With few exceptions, changing the drag setting during the fight risks a breakoff. As you tighten the drag, it's difficult to measure the precise amount. A better system suggests that you use your hands to apply additional resistance. The thumb can slow a revolving spool reel and the fingers fit nicely around the spool on a spinning model. If the fish should surge, you can remove the extra pressure instantly.

Unknowing anglers usually try to stop a long, sustained run by tightening the drag, particularly when it appears as if there may not be enough line on the spool. As the diameter of line on the spool decreases, the amount of drag increases. If you tighten the adjustment, you compound the problem and will probably regale your friends with tales of the monster that got away. The proper action centers on loosening the drag adjustment until the fish stops and you can regain some of the line.

Bonefish earned their reputation by streaking across shallow flats when hooked. Too tight a drag curtails this ability and deprives one of the sport's attraction. The opposite problem faces the fisherman who must stop a husky denizen from reaching the sanctuary of a wreck, reef, or other structure. As one veteran explains drag in those situations, "I set it on exterminate and play tug-of-war." If the fish reaches the underwater haven, it's all over. Crank down on the drag (within sensible limits) and hope for the best.

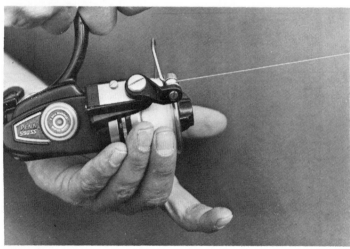

Cup the spool when additional drag pressure is needed, instead of playing with the dial. That way you can instantly release the pressure and stay within the guidelines of a proper setting.

THE STRIKE

Reacting to a strike requires a pair of instant decisions: when to set the hook and the best method for burying the barb. Certain bait-stealers are so slick that regulars report they set the hook just before the fish bites the bait. With most species, you have much more time to react than you suspect. The somewhat reflexive action of rearing back on the rod the moment you feel something on the other end frequently costs you a fish.

Rod holders rank as one of the most effective hooking devices and they don't move. The fish moves off with the bait until the line becomes tight and its own swimming motion forces the hook into its skin.

Monofilament line boasts at least 25 percent stretch.

That's the cushioning effect that makes it so forgiving when fighting a heavyweight. If a fish grabbed a bait 40 feet from you, you would have to sweep the rod 10 feet just to take out the stretch and the slack.

No matter how or when you set the hook, the first rule dictates that the line between you and the fish be absolutely tight with as much stretch as possible removed. At the same time, the rod tip should point directly at the spot where the line enters the water or at the fish. Once you accomplish these two requirements, the rest becomes refinement of technique.

Your first instinct in the hook-setting process should focus on turning the reel handle as fast as you can and dropping the rod tip so that it points at the fish. When you feel the line come tight and begin to strain against the drag, you can follow with short, sharp sweeps of the rod.

If the fish strikes a bait and starts to move off quickly, you may want to drop the rod tip and wait for the line to pull drag before reacting. In a chum slick, serious anglers watch the line. When it starts to move, they push the rod tip toward the fish, wait for the solid feel of a moving fish, and then set the hook. No matter what you do, the line must be tight or you merely alert the fish that something is amiss.

Unless the line is straight up and down, striking sideways makes more sense than vertically lifting the rod. At any distance, the side strike achieves a straighter pull and it keeps the bait or lure in front of the fish if you should miss. That becomes particularly important with surface lures and baits trolled on top. Lock your arms against your body and rotate your legs and hips to generate power. You can't drive a nail with one blow from a hammer and the same argument applies to a hookset. Try three or four rapid strikes.

Knowing when to strike forms the second part of the equation. Timing can be critical. If a fish hits an artificial lure

Monofilament line boasts at least 25 percent stretch, a cushioning effect that makes it forgiving when fighting a heavyweight. A sharp skipper keeps the boat trolling after a hook-up until he believes the initial stretch is out and the iron is well imbedded. That was the case during this Bahamas blue marlin double header.

Live baiters go into freespool when a fish takes a bait. When it's time to set the hook, throw the reel in gear and crank the handle until the line comes tight. Strike the fish with several short jabs.

THE KNOCKOUT PUNCH

Angler error or tackle failure prove to be the two primary causes of pulled hooks or broken lines. The longer your quarry swims around, the greater the risk of a mistake. Dance and spar with your quarry until you can deliver that knockout punch and bring a tired competitor alongside the boat or drag it on the sand. The instant you set the hook expect that critter to bolt away without looking back. Some species strain the reel with sizzling runs for long distances, while others crash dive toward the bottom. Your drag has been pre-set to handle the initial surge. If you clamp down and try to stop the run, the line will surely break. Enjoy it, be patient, and wait until the fish stops.

By holding the rod at a 45 degree angle to the water, you force the fish to pull against extra pressure. If the fish is particularly large, exceptionally fast, capable of long runs, and your line is relatively light, drop the rod tip and point it at your quarry. This reduces the amount of pre-set drag and helps to compensate for the additional resistance caused by pulling a long length of line through the water at high speed.

If you're aboard a boat, you should be thinking of following that heavyweight so you can counter the run and begin to regain line. Don't steer a course straight toward the fish. Instead, trace the path of the line until you are back on a direct pull with the fish. Tests show that large bellies in lines create excessive pressure causing breakage. When you can't keep up with the fish or if you're on shore and the amount of line on the spool begins to dwindle, back off on the drag adjustment to help relieve the additional reistance.

Stand toe-to-toe with your adversary and slug it out. You can't let that animal rest for a second. If it is not taking line off the reel, you're battling to regain it. Pumping defines the preferred technique. Beginners try to winch a fish toward them with the reel, ignoring the rod. Instead, lift the rod slowly and smoothly, pulling the fish toward you. Start the rod tip right at the surface of the water or parallel to it. Raise the rod until it scribes an angle with the surface of about 75 degrees. Then, reel quickly to regain the controlled slack as you drop the rod tip. Repeat the procedure again and again until the fish is alongside the boat.

These long, slow pumps work when your quarry remains on the surface or just below it. If a fish slugs it out in the depths, you have to pump it to the surface. A better technique focuses on the short pump. In this scenario, you move the rod a foot or two, take a half turn of the reel handle as you lower the rod, and repeat the excercise. Veterans build a rhythm without a hint of a pause between strokes. If you do hesitate, the fish turns around again and starts back down. Once you get a fish coming toward you, keep the pressure steady.

Line twist becomes the nemesis of those who battle fish on spinning tackle. If you turn the reel handle without regaining line, you put twist in it. With a reel that boasts a 5:1 gear ratio, a single revolution of the handle without gaining line puts five twists in it. Multiply this by the number of times it happens and the line will be unfishable. To counter the problem, be sure you pump the fish, turning the handle only when you drop the rod on the down stroke. If your line does get twisted, cut off all terminal tackle and troll it behind the boat for a few minutes. That should remove the twist.

simply reel as fast as you can until you can feel strong tension against the line. Then, set the hook. The same approach applies to topwater baits as well.

With bait, the game takes on more variables. The best clue comes when a fish starts to move off steadily. A fish may pick up a bait, move away slowly, stop, and then move at a faster pace. In that time frame, your quarry picked up the offering, turned it around to swallow it head first, blew the water in its mouth out through the gills, and swallowed the meal. Particularly with a live bait, you have to allow time for that to happen. Many species have crushers in the back of their mouths and will toss a bait or lure back there first, giving you plenty of time to react.

If you're fishing live bait (and sometimes dead bait), the preferred technique lies in freespooling the bait once it is picked up. That allows your quarry to move off without feeling any resistance. How long you wait depends on the situation and your own experience. When you decide to set the hook, throw the reel in gear and wait for the line to come tight or crank the reel handle. If a fish jumps while you are dropping back with a bait, it knows there is something wrong and is trying to get rid of it. Put the reel in gear instantly and reel as fast as you can until the line comes tight.

Any angler who isn't expecting a big fish to make a mad boat-side dash is in for plenty of heartache. Be prepared to counter such actions. This angler has just finessed a big shark to the surface on light-tackle, yet he knows the battle is far from over. Notice how he's cutting the playing distance around the boat to stay out of trouble.

Many species put up the most stubborn resistance a mere 50-feet or less from the rod tip. They turn their bodies broadside to the source of the pressure and one can stand there with a bent rod for an inordinate amount of time without gaining an inch of line. No matter how many times you try, you must keep attempting to move the head of the fish. Side pressure often does the trick. If the fish is heading to the right, sweep the rod to the left, keeping it low and parallel to the water. Hold this reversal of pressure until the fish turns to counter it. Then, reverse the rod and sweep it to the right. It's similar to tacking a sailboat into the wind.

Keep changing the direction of pull so that the fish has to adjust to it. If the head of your quarry points away from you, stick the rod tip in the water and pull back. You are trying to disorient the fish and turn it over. It's surprising how a big fish can be upended with this method.

The same theory applies to a fish that lingers a few dozen feet below the surface and refuses to budge. Try changing angles by moving the boat. If that fails, rely on short pumping. You may only gain a few inches of line and lose a foot on the next attempt, but the process must continue.

THE LAST ROUND

You can bet a week's pay that any fish will surge away from the boat the first time you try to land it. The sudden burst shocks the line and can snap it easily if you don't react. When your quarry makes that final bid for freedom, drop the rod tip and point it right at the fish. That will minimize the amount of drag and help to cushion the blow. Once the reel

spool begins to yield line, you can lift the rod and work th[e] fish back to the boat or beach.

If you plan to release your catch, focus on keeping it i[n] the water while you remove the hook or cut the leader. Th[e] less you handle any sea creature, the greater its chances [of] survival. Handling removes the protective mucous from th[e] fish's skin, making it susceptible to infection. At the sam[e] time, you don't want the animal to thrash violently or beat i[t-] self against the side of the boat. To prevent this, you ma[y] have to use a net or slip a release gaff through the membran[e] in the lower jaw.

An impressive number of release tools are on the marke[t] and all of them work. A pair of pliers can do wonders an[d] you can often remove a hook by turning it upside down wit[h] a gaff. If a fish is hooked deeply, don't try to work the hoo[k] loose. Simply cut the leader as close to the mouth as possibl[e.] The fish will survive very nicely. Too many anglers kill shark[s] and barracuda because it seems like the macho thing to d[o.] Diminished numbers of these species make it prudent to r[e-] lease them. A barracuda can be handled easily, but shark[s] prove more tricky. The best procedure with a shark is to c[ut] the leader.

Tailers make it relatively easy to handle larger specie[s.] You slip the loop of the tailer over the fish's tail and pu[ll] sharply. Once the tailer engages, be sure to lift the tail out [of] the water immediately. Otherwise, that heavyweight will dra[g] you around the boat. With a tailer and a pair of gloves, yo[u] can handle most fish, remove the hook, and turn them loos[e.]

If you decide to keep your quarry, a net or gaff make[s]

anding easier and safer. Place the net in the water at a 45 degree angle and lead the fish into it. Remember that fish cannot swim backward, so once you have them moving toward the net, it's easy to swim them into it. Don't let the person with the net make wild stabs. You run the risk of having the net hit the line or leader and the fish will be lost.

Gaffs demand a bit more skill. The easiest technique starts by placing the gaff in the water and slipping it under the fish from behind the leader. Then, lift sharply and the point should bury in the underside of the fish. You have the option of reaching across the fish's back and pulling toward you. If you put the gaff in front of the leader, you'll probably break the line or pull the hook.

Knowing where to gaff a fish is important. If you hit a species with teeth such as a wahoo in the middle, it will slash like a snake and could cause serious injury. You have to control the head. Before you gaff a fish, open the cooler or fish-box so you can drop it inside quickly and close the lid. Gaffing demands a positive action. When you make your move, it has to be swift, true, and powerful.

Most fish species have some form of protective device. Teeth are the most obvious, but fins, spines, and even razor sharp edges on gill plates can cause serious injury if you don't handle the critter correctly. Know the fish before you reach for it; wear gloves whenever possible; and be sure you get a firm grip. The last thing you want is a hook in your hand and in the fish at the same time.

When you land a fish with net or gaff, pick your time. If the fish isn't ready or you can't get it in the right position, have the angler swim it around once more. Keep doing this until you get the shot.

Stay alert and keep a tight line: any slack is a major advantage for a hot fish.

Gaffing fish requires a cool head. If you're shooting for the shoulder, keep the gaff behind the leader. If possible, lead the fish into the cooler. You can always retrieve the lure when it settles down.

Sailfish and smaller marlin can be handled by grabbing their bills with gloved hands. It's easier to do this if you move the boat ahead slightly and try to grab the bill when it is just under the surface. A billfish can slash quickly and with tremendous power, making it essential that you pick the precise moment to make your move.

Grasp the bill with your thumbs pointing at each other. If the fish should thrash or try to jump, your arms will guide the fish clear of your body. Handling a big fish requires skill and knowledge. You always have the option of cutting the leader without touching the fish.

If you spend enough days on the water, count on tangling with the trophy fish of your dreams. It will happen suddenly and without warning. Most anglers suddenly become overly cautious, trying desperately to land the fish by using the minimum amount of pressure. They don't want to risk breaking the line. In the process, the chances of tackle failure or angler error increase dramatically. The bigger your adversary, the more important it becomes to slug it out with everything you have. Baby the fish and you can kiss it goodbye. That doesn't mean you can get careless, but you have to pressure it into submission. And, if you release that trophy, it brings a particularly warm feeling that words fail to describe.

Sailfish and smaller marlin can be handled by grabbing their bill with gloved hands. Remove the hook, or cut the leader if it's deep and send the fish on its way.

Try to be brief when releasing a fish. The less you handle it, the better of it will fare.

CATCHING FISH WITH ELECTRONICS

Today's offshore fisherman can't survive without loran or GPS. Mark a productive area and you can return to it the following morning. Getting to fish can be as easy as subscribing to an ocean forecasting service (which discloses the whereabouts of temperature breaks and fishy areas) and plugging in their loran coordinates.

ARRIVING ON THE MONEY

There's no denying that Loran-C is one of the greatest tools available to the marine angler. When the system was introduced to the boating public at competitive prices it gave even the most novice skippers the ability to navigate precisely to any destination, if they had the waypoints (WP).

In the "good old days" finding a prime piece of bottom hinged on lining up range markers or embarking on a timed, calculated run. If the piece of bottom was close to land with plenty of reference points, locating it wasn't that difficult. Needless to say, finding far off spots on limited ranges were challenging and dependant on bright, clear days. And if you weren't good at calculating your boat's speed over a known distance at a specific rpm and factoring in variables such as seas, current and excess weight, executing this procedure often proved to be nothing more than a boat ride.

With a quality loran, spots that were once the domain of a handful of sharp skippers became accessible to anyone who had a unit. What's more, traveling to distant spots and fishing destinations became a much securer proposition. Now boaters even have access to yet another electronic navigation system: Global Positioning System (GPS). In a nut shell, GPS is a satellite navigation system that's supported by at least 18 satellites orbiting the earth, with at least four in direct view

continuously (a latitude/longitude fix is obtainable with three satellites). A receiver determines a vessel's position by calculating its distance from the transmitters by factoring the period of delay between transmission time and reception. Positions read in Lat/Lon, but quality units convert these into Time Differences (TDs). Similar to loran, GPS continuously updates your position and speed (much quicker than loran at less than a second), displays a vessel's heading, steering guidance, distance and time to go and has considerable waypoint memory. Two important GPS advantages are that adverse weather won't affect it and it's world wide. That means it supports captains and anglers in areas where loran coverage is "iffy" or totally non-existent. Think of the benefits of locating and returning to areas with major bait and fish concentrations off popular destinations such as Costa Rica, Panama, Venezuela, Ecuador, Mexico, far reaches of the Bahamas or Caribbean, etc. If one captain lucks into fish, and the fleet hasn't found them, he can accurately direct a buddy or stable-mate to his whereabouts, providing the other boat has GPS capabilities. It can be a God-send in returning to major ledges, bottom obstructions or fish migrations, eliminating much of the guess work that currently exists.

Loran, on the other hand, is a pulsed, low frequency, radio-navigational system dependent on a chain of three to five shore based transmitting stations. Each chain is comprised of a Master and at least two Secondary transmitting stations, which releases an association of pulses at specified Group Repetition Intervals (GRI). The loran C chain for a designated area is determined electronically by the individualized GRI, with some nine series applying to U.S. regions.

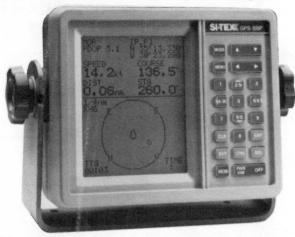

GPS is a satellite navigation system. Similar to loran, it gives a speed and position update (much quicker than loran at less than a second), vessel heading, steering guidance, distance and time to go. The better models also have plotter capabilities. Coverage is world wide because of their satellite dependency, and adverse weather won't affect their performance.

A loran can be loaded (memory) with proven fishing spots. An angler can then formulate a circuit and hit each area as he moves offshore, budgeting valuable fishing time. A quality loran offers plenty of memory (with some models boasting an incredible 200-waypoint capability), speed display, mileage log and the ability to be interfaced with an autopilot or other onboard electronics.

The Master station transmitter identifies and synchronizes the loran C chain. Pulsed signals transmitted by two Secondary stations are synchronously timed with the Master station. The synchronized pulses are then transmitted at precise time intervals and processed by the loran C unit to measure the distance in time required for these pulses to reach the shipboard receiver from each of the transmitters. The difference in time is sensibly referred to as Time Differences (TD). The TDs appear on a digital readout display, giving the boater's current position.

The best available secondaries should be selected. Each Master-secondary pair produces one Line of Position (LOP). For accuracy, choose secondaries that provide LOP crossing angles that are close to 90 degrees. After locking in the desired secondaries, the unit will display the vessel's location. A captain can even visualize his approximate position on a loran-overprinted navigational chart by locating the point where the two LOPs intersect.

AT THE GROUNDS

GPS isn't intended to replace loran and both actually compliment each other in navigation and finding fish. For instance, anglers that have accumulated "fixes" on hot fishing spots can store many of them into a unit's memory. By programming them in an orderly fashion they'll have a circuit of numbers to run during the day. Valuable fishing time can be spent at these points, not running around trying to locate a good area. Gulf of Mexico and Atlantic bottom anglers searching for groupers, snappers and scamp have circuits comprised of rockpiles, irregular bottom, shelves and wrecks that attract these species. They'll set forth and hit the ones closest to shore first before they're pressured by others, giving each spot about 15-minutes to produce before working their way farther offshore.

Recording the hot areas during the day gives the offshore angler the option of returning directly to them the following day. Gamefish concentrated in certain areas can stay somewhat close to these zones for a limited period, if bait supply, weather and currents remain stable. There have been plenty of offshore anglers who have scored well with tuna and billfish, only to return to the same areas the following day and hit them again. However, if you're in transit to a primary destination, record all potential areas with bait, rips, a color change or water temperature variations. They could serve as back-ups if the main point doesn't produce.

Programming the coordinates of any promising structure along their fishing route can keep trollers over prime areas. Similar to the bottom anglers who create and run down a circuit of prime beds, the trollers can work in a similar fashion. This system is especially effective for trolling around wrecks and natural bottom.

KNOW WHERE YOU'VE BEEN

Some loran and GPS units have plotter capabilities. A plotter is a visual aid that helps a navigator pinpoint his vessel's position relative to its intended track. For example, a boater leaving Miami enroute to Bimini, Bahamas, will program both destinations into the unit. By switching to this function and fine tuning the ranges to include the approximate 50-mile gap, he can actually monitor his path between the two points (illustrated by a line). It's a great addition for navigation, but a plotter can also be an invaluable fishing aid. By defining and entering boundaries along a wall or drop-off, hump, reef line or even open ocean, an angler can monitor his trolling pattern and effectively execute the targeted area. He'll be able to concentrate on specific areas and have the ability to see how much ground is actually being covered. By keeping track of his trolling pattern he'll be certain to maintain a "fresh" course and not continually duplicate his passes, that is unless they produce fish.

AND WHERE YOU'RE AT

One of the most important advantages of loran and GPS, and the most overlooked, is safety. If a boater were to develop trouble many miles from shore or was in a life threatening situation, reading his coordinates to another vessel or the Coast Guard will guarantee that they get their precise whereabouts. They'll punch in the numbers and hone in on what should be a quick and efficient rescue. There's no need to try and estimate your position, which could be way off the mark if you didn't accurately compensate for current and wind direction. Besides, very few minds can think clearly in a critical situation.

Storing the coordinates of several inlets or passes within striking range of both home and destination ports gives an angler the latitude of skirting adverse weather. If threatening weather blocks his primary port he can choose a passage on either side as an escape route. Plenty of experienced boaters have a memory bank logging inlets as far as 40-miles on both sides of a primary port.

THE UNDERWATER WORLD

A fishfinder is an angler's view of the underwater world. He can spend a fortune on a boat and tackle and still be at a serious disadvantage if he can't effectively monitor the water column. The sharp angler knows that there's more to just watching the surface, and he'll invest a pretty penny on a machine that thoroughly covers the depths he fishes most. Fortunately, there are quality machines available for most budgets. Liquid Crystal Display (LCD) machines are a popular option because they use no paper. Images are created by tiny pixels or squares, with the better units containing more pixels per square inch to illustrate a remarkably sharp picture. Most models have depth capabilities to around 500-feet. The color video sounder, a main-stay aboard large sportfishing boats, is becoming popular on vessels in the 23

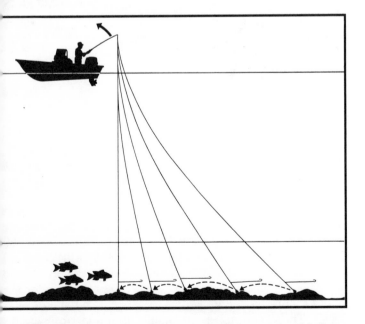

A fishfinder is an angler's link to the underwater world. Some benthic species aren't keen on feeding far from their lairs. Sink a bait several feet away and you'll be burning daylight. Drop a bait on top of them and your next worry may be getting a bruiser up from the ocean floor.

through 30-foot range. This is attributed to the quality equipment available at attractive prices and also their compact size. Models for the recreational angler have maximum depth capabilities nearing 2,500 feet, while those geared to commercial fishing exceed 3,000-feet.

One important feature is their ability to zoom in on a selected area. For example, if fish are marked near 50-feet, and the current scale reads between 0 and 100-feet, you can mag-

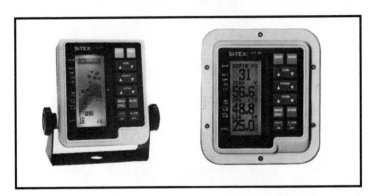

LCD machines rely on tiny pixels or squares to illustrate all that's below the transom. The more "pixels" a manufacturer can squeeze into a square inch, the more detailed the picture. These highly popular units require no paper. Depending upon the model, they also display bottom depth, surface water temperature, boat speed, distance traveled, and split-screen features. Top-of-the-line models now enable an angler to scroll the display back to review the most recent conditions. And for maximum repeatability you can recall up to four pages from memory to aid in returning to your most productive fishing spots.

nify that zone and get a better idea as to their size (and perhaps species) by entering 40-feet as an upper limit and 60-feet as the lower limit. Bottom anglers are notorious for adjusting their units to magnify the last ten feet of the water column to pick-up on fish which may be in a lair or hugging the bottom. They can also distinguish pockets of bait, which mean gamefish shouldn't be that far off.

Scrutinizing the entire water column helps determine the pace of the fishing. Conditions such as water temperatures and bait concentrations may keep fish at certain levels. Just because they may be marked only 20-feet down doesn't mean they'll come up for a bait. If deep jiggers are marking pelagics in the middle of the water column, they'll do much better by shortening their window to that particular zone. Ditto downrigger trollers and live baiters.

Anglers who realize the importance of reading the water column benefit tremendously from some of the latest fishfinder technology. There are machines with split screen capabilities that automatically fix on bottom and illustrate it as a continuous flat line to simplify the hunt for bottom hugging fish or bait, in addition to depicting the natural contour. This feature, incidentally, is impervious to even sea-induced motion. You can even magnify and scan a specific portion of the water column while simultaneously retaining the normal presentation.

Audible fish alarms are big assets, and the multi levels of color intensity found in video sounders even alert you to specific size fish. When you consider the other features like keel alarms, speed and water temperature and digital depth readings, it's easy to understand the vital role such a unit plays.

Selecting the right transducer is crucial to a fishfinder's performance. To get the maximum output the transducer's operating frequency should reflect the primary depths the unit is intended for. If most of its use is deeper than 300-feet, a transducer with an operating frequency of 50 kHz provides

Split-screen capabilities enable one to depict the bottom contour in its natural form and also as a continuous flat line to simplify the hunt for bottom hugging fish or bait. This feature, in a quality machine, is impervious to sea-induced motion. Some models also have a plotter and a dual frequency option.

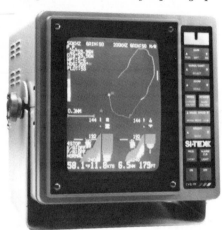

Commercial fishermen and hard-core blue water anglers prefer a large screen color sounder that packs enough power to penetrate 3,000 foot depths. What's the advantage of reading so deep? To find irregular bottom contours such as peaks, depressions or sharp ledges in the ocean floor – areas that may hold bait and possibly displace them under a hard current. Bait and thermoclines are also picked up.

the necessary punch to penetrate these depths. In waters shallower than 300-feet, a 200 kHz provides the high resolution that's needed for a superbly detailed picture. However, there are dual frequency combinations available for those who frequent both deep and shallow waters, whereas a 120 kHz transducer offers the best of both worlds in a single package. Consult the company's technician as to the best area and means of mounting your transducer. If it's mounted properly and subject to little interference, there should be no problem realizing the unit's maximum depth capabilities.

A water surface temperature gauge is a small, yet shouldn't-be-without item. Successful anglers religiously

monitor them for breaks or fluctuations in sea water temperature, which could yield productive fishing along their edges. They're especially instrumental off the northeast where warm water eddies (circulating portions of a warm water current that break away from the main flow) are sought. They're equally important to the inshore fisherman

Small boaters can also share the advantages of a color sounder. There are models that come with a six-inch screen and many features of the larger machines. A good six-inch sounder shouldn't have a problem operating in over 1,000 feet of water.

Combining the capabilities of loran or GPS and a quality color machine will make you that much more efficient when searching out major offshore gamefish.

A LESSON IN SAFETY

Boaters are well aware of the merits of a VHF, that high frequency radio operating on a "line of sight" principle. They use them to learn fish whereabouts and what they're striking best. They're also a life-line to shore or another boater and lend a secure feeling while traveling across a bay, sound or ocean. Those serious about their communications carry a secondary or back-up radio rigged to a totally separate system, in the event an antennae is damaged or a radio goes on the blink.

Despite the quality and dependability of modern radios

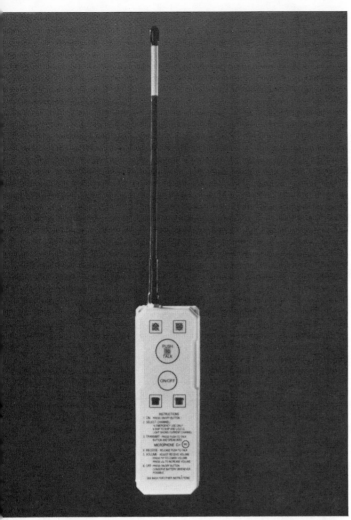

a hand held VHF is a smart investment. In the event of a boating mishap where the batteries have become submerged, that vessel's communication capabilities will be gone. By carrying a hand held VHF, the distressed boater still has a chance at raising another vessel.

The situation doesn't even have to be that severe. For instance, an angler could be anchored or drifting at night only to discover that his batteries were drained. It could have been the console or bait lights, stereo, live well pump or a combination of all of the above that left him stranded. Dead batteries mean no starting power, no bilge pumps, and no VHF capabilities. Unless he possess a hand held radio to notify someone, he'll become dependant on another boat venturing by or the flare kit. There are a number of top notch VHF radios and even one that's intended solely for survival applications. The latter is a high visibility yellow radio carrying only channels 16 and 6. The button controls are large and easy to read and the radio automatically tunes to channel 16 with the volume at its highest level. The immersion proof VHF, generating a 1/2 watt of power, floats and should be purchased and strapped immediately to a life vest. It's a recommended addition to a regular hand held.

A new, fully waterproof emergency VHF radio has hit the market. The high visibility yellow radio carries only channels 16 and 6. It turns on automatically to channel 16 with the volume at its highest level, which makes it easier for a boater in a life threatening situation to raise help.

A hand held VHF will not only keep you informed on the action, it'll come in handy if your vessel develops battery trouble.

Strobes flash a brilliant xenon light as high as 60 times a minute for as long as nine hours, transmitting a highly visible rescue signal. What's more, they're waterproof, shock resistant, activated by a push button and recognized as an emergency distress signal. Many of these strobes are meant to be attached to a PFD so you won't have to hunt for them in an emergency.

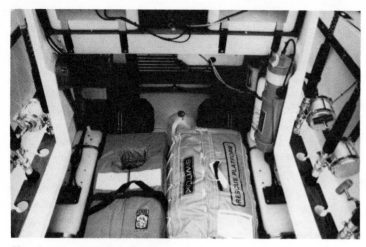

Here's a peek inside the console of a well prepared center console. Notice the PFDs, Rescue Platform and 121.5 MHz EPIRB – all ready for quick deployment.

THE EPIRB INFLUENCE

The Emergency Position Indicating Radio Beacon (EPIRB) has become state of the art and extremely efficient in aiding mariners in crisis situations. The 406 Megahertz (MHz) system is designed specifically to interact with a network of at least four fully operational U.S. satellites and three Soviet spacecraft navigation satellites. Part of an international co-operation to provide satellite assistance for search and rescue operations, those of both the Soviets and United States have COSPAS/SARSAT (Search And Rescue Satellite-Aided Tracking) payloads to receive these signals. The satellites cover the world in less than four hours. The COSPAS (Soviet acronym for Space System for Search of Distressed Vessels)/SARSAT effort is also comprised of Canada, France, Bulgaria, Finland, Norway, Sweden and the United Kingdom.

This translates into a modern, highly efficient, worldwide means to receive, store and dispatch a rescue signal. Let's compare the new system to a conventional EPIRB transmitting on the low power 121.5 MHz frequency. The 121.5 does have satellite capabilities but there has to be mutual visibility between the satellite, the beacon and the ground station (LUT – local user terminal) for a minimum of two satellite passes before a position composite is obtained. If transmission is hindered, you're bound to wait longer for another opportunity. There's no method of storing a signal and this system is slanted more toward aircraft and commercial ships that may be monitoring the 121.5 MHz frequency.

The 406 MHz signal is stored instantly aboard the satellite and bounced down to a LUT, if in line with it, or later relayed to the next available one, thus covering the entire earth's surface and facilitating a quicker rescue response. Each 406 MHz EPIRB contains a vital identification code which is transmitted by the satellite to a LUT, which then transfers it for decoding to NOAA's Data Base Registry in Suitland, Maryland (within the U.S. jurisdiction). The information reveals the type of vessel, owner's name, address and phone number (obtained from the registration card). If one is lit off, a phone call from the Coast Guard helps determine if the signal is an accident or a true emergency before deploying limited manpower on an expensive search and rescue mission.

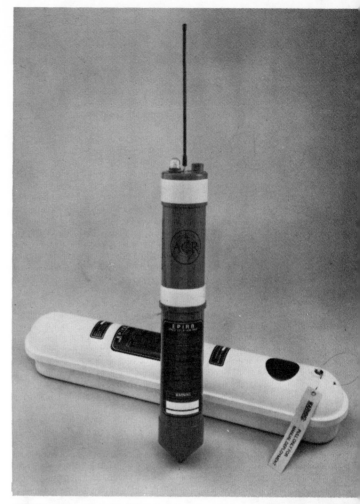

The Emergency Position Indicating Radio Beacon (EPIRB) is now capable of interacting with a network of navigation satellites. In a nut shell, the signal of this 406 MHz system will hit a satellite, which instantly stores it and then bounces it down to a local user terminal (LUT). If it's of U.S. origin, the LUT transfers it to NOAA's Data Base Registry in Maryland where it will be decoded (each 406 MHz EPIRB contains a vital identification code). Rescue response time is dramatically shortened with the 406 MHz unit. No offshore boater should overlook this insurance.

A much smaller "window" of location accuracy is another benefit of the 406 MHz. In contrast to the typical five and ten nautical miles of the 121.5 MHz system (off the satellite), the 406 MHz performs to within three miles. The 406 MHz is also complimented with a 121.5 MHz transmitter (low power transmission) for accurate homing capabilities during conventional search and rescue operations. They're available in Category I, activated automatically or by manual release, and Category II, manually activated.

The 121.5 MHz EPIRB is still a worthy unit and very popular among boaters on limited budgets (costing between $250 and $600). There was a recent incident where a boat capsized in rough seas 300-miles south of Bermuda. A class B EPIRB worked for him. Its signal was picked up instantly by a satellite and relayed to the Coast Guard, whose aircraft honed in on the signal two hours later. A Norwegian tanker after being notified by the Coast Guard, picked the skipper from the seas several hours later. He was in fine shape and credits that EPIRB with saving his life.

Rods and reels may add to the angler's enjoyment of the sport, but fish focus on the line, leader, hook, sinker, and swivel. These vital elements of the total tackle system seldom receive adequate attention. If you plan to fool finicky customers on a regular basis, your approach must go beyond simply tossing something in the water and hoping for the best. Every element of terminal tackle must be selected carefully and put together in a meaningful sequence.

THE BOTTOM LINE

All fishing line is not the same. As a starting point, recognize that premium quality monofilament may cost a little more, but it pays off in performance. Maintaining a relatively uniform diameter and more rigid manufacturing standards

Premium fishing line may cost a bit more, but the investment will pay dividends when you hook up with those tough-to-manage gamefish. Tournament grade lines are manufactured to break at slightly below their designated ratings, the choice of serious record hunters.

add to the price. Making line represents a complex process in which several properties must be balanced. That's why monofilament makers must come up with an acceptable compromise. Stretch, limpness, diameter, abrasion resistance, and other factors relate to each other. If you change one, the others may be affected.

Labels on line spools don't tell the whole story, but they make a sensible starting point. Stated breaking strength helps you match the line to the rod and reel. Actual breaking strength may differ significantly from the stated one. By law, the line cannot test less than the number printed on the label. It may, however, test much more. As an example, the line on a spool labelled 10-pound test may actually break at 13 pounds or even 15 pounds. It cannot break at 9.9 pounds unless the label states that it is tournament grade guaranteed to part at less than 10 pounds.

The problem with a tournament line lies in a manufacturer's ability to maintain consistency and that's not easy. It would be wonderful if tournament grade 12 pound would break at 11.8 pounds. Don't count on it. You may discover to your dismay that 12 pound tournament grade actually breaks at 8 pounds or 9 pounds.

A few labels contain information on diameter, but most mono makers have tended to avoid listing it. The finer the diameter, the better the line should cast and the more naturally it might present a bait or lure. Knowledgeable anglers are now comparing diameter with breaking strength in an attempt to pick the strongest combination.

You won't find any measurement of limpness, abrasion resistance, stretch, or the other factors on the label. Usually, a limper line is easier to handle and often casts better than a stiffer one. Recognize that abrasion resistance represents a built-in property and is not a function of limpness or stiffness. Some fishermen erroneously believe that stiff monofilament is more abrasion resistant.

Another misconception centers on stretch. The typical monofilament stretches about 25 percent when under load. Anglers often view this as a negative characteristic and, in a way, there is some validity in that statement. Actually, the stretch in mono makes it very forgiving. Many more fish would be lost if it weren't for the stretch. That's the cushion that covers one's mistakes when fighting an angry critter.

Braided Dacron stretches less than 10 percent and has become the line of choice in a handful of fishing situations such as tangling with giant tuna. Pumping a huge fish from the depths of the sea proves much easier with Dacron. In the tradeoff, however, an angler must be careful because he has sacrificed the safety cushion of stretch.

Monofilament line should be changed frequently. Excessive heat and the ultra-violet rays of the sun will destroy line. Abrasion becomes another culprit, weakening the single filament by nicking it. You'll find that it doesn't take much abrasion to significantly weaken a section of line. Check for abrasion by running the line through your fingertips. If it feels rough, cut off the bad section and re-tie the terminal gear.

Monofilament now comes in an assortment of decorator colors ranging from pinks and blues to greens and clear. Regardless of shade, all monofilament can be seen underwater. Fluorescent lines prove to be brighter and much easier to see below the surface than the standard tones.

Anglers often believe rather strongly that line of one color outperforms all the others. The problem is that fishermen can't agree on which color. If you have looked at lines underwater, you begin to understand that visibility changes based on water clarity, depth, light patterns, and so forth. Background probably ranks as the primary factor. The color of the background and the quality and amount of light striking it often determines which colors will be less visible. It's still worth experimenting with different colors until you find the one in which you have the most confidence.

LEADER LOGIC

A leader is a length of heavier material between the end of the fishing line and the hook or lure, offering protection against sharp teeth or abrasion from the fish's body. The key lies in choosing the minimum leader that will handle the assignment in terms of material, diameter, and length. Those

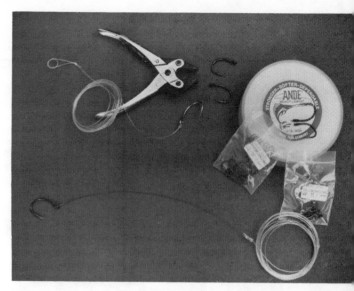

You should always choose the lightest leader system that can get the job done. Monofilament is less visible and it doesn't r a bait or lure of its action. Toothy species often require a meta lic one. Try adding a small wire trace to a monofilament lea er; you'll receive the necessary protection without over-gunnir the system.

three factors spell out the entire subject of leader logic.

Experience points to the fact that a monofilament lea er usually outperforms one made from wire or cable. Tha doesn't mean that other materials won't work, but merely i dicates the odds lean toward the mono. Bluefish boast aw some dentures and the big slammers can easily chop throug relatively heavy mono. If you go for a wire leader, you'll ge fewer strikes most days. It's a tradeoff, but one worth co sidering. Do you use mono and run the risk of an occasion cutoff or should you stick to wire and worry about fewe strikes?

In southern waters, the king mackerel also has a mout full of razor blades. Wire is the order of the day for most ar glers, but those who fish with light mono fool a lot more fish The decision is yours. We're simply trying to point out the di ferences.

At one time, every offshore fishing boat carried coils 49-strand aircraft cable for big game sport. Eventually, the

Some anglers swear that fish can distinguish certain line colors, and each coastal region seems to have their preference. Yellowtail fans, for example, swear that pink is the least visible.

A monofilament leader will catch toothy species if the lure long enough to keep the two separated. This bluefish couldn bite beyond the rubber tubing.

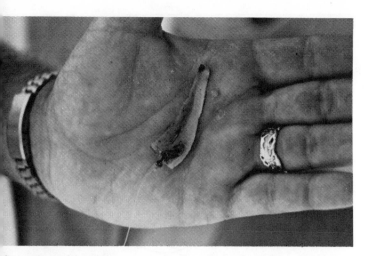

Sometimes it's necessary to tie directly to the fishing line. This approach is for fish that are especially reluctant to feed.

learned that they did much better with heavy monofilament. Marlin trollers now rig their lures and baits with mono as heavy as 700-pound test rather than the cable of yesteryear. The primary use for cable today is for large sharks that show no mercy on mono.

When you do need wire, the first choice is single strand, stainless steel. You decide whether you prefer coffee-colored or bright wire. There are arguments for both colors. This does the job on barracuda, smaller sharks, wahoo, and other toothy critters. Trollers sometimes rely on braided wire because it is more flexible and does not kink. If single strand wire kinks, cut it off and tie on a new piece. A kink weakens it dramatically.

Single strand should be attached using the haywire twist, making certain you break off the tag end and do not cut it with pliers. If you break the end, it will not leave a burr that can tear up your hands later. Sleeves and crimps work best on cable, heavy mono, and braided wire, although light braided wire can be knotted.

Heavier is not better. If you can land enough fish with a 50 pound leader, don't think that 80 provides a better cushion. Leader diameter often makes a difference, so you want the smallest diameter consistent with the task. That holds across the board for monofilament, single strand wire, cable, and anything else you might use. Go with the smaller diameter and it will eventually pay off. Tuna fishermen learn early in the game how important leader diameter can be and the lesson transcends most other types of fishing.

Leader length forms the final leg of the triangle. You want the shortest leader possible within sensible parameters. If 6 inches of single strand wire will adequately offer protection against fish with sharp dentures, a foot of leader becomes a negative factor.

Consider the option of combining wire, braided wire, or even cable with monofilament. With the first two, a small swivel makes an excellent connector or you can tie the two materials together using a knot system. Cable requires crimps. In a typical setup, you need a leader to stretch across the body of certain fish as protection against abrasion. That animal may have sharp teeth, but it will only take a short length of wire to deal with that problem. Attach the mono to the wire and you just made the perfect leader.

Rigging properly takes both thought and technique. If you're going to cast, you want the connection between leader and line or lighter and heavier leader to remain beyond the tiptop of the rod. That way, the knot doesn't get pulled through the tiptop on every cast. Before tying the final knots, measure the distance carefully.

If you big game fish from a center-console or a cuddy, you may want to consider a leader system that eliminates swivels and allows you to reel an oversized fish right to the boat. Crews aboard towering sportfishing yachts rig long leaders and then "wire" the fish when they can grab the extended leader. That's a dangerous procedure under the best of conditions and often difficult to accomplish on a small boat. By knotting the leader segments together and eliminating the swivel, you can crank your quarry right up to the rodtip without worrying about a wire man. The same system makes sense on any boat, but the concept remains tougher to sell on the big boats with two and three-man crews.

GETTING THE POINT

Man has made fish hooks almost since the millenium of time. They appear simple enough with a shank, bend, barb, and point, but thousands of patterns and countless sizes are still manufactured commercially. Unfortunately, sizes and even shape varies among hook makers, eliminating any semblance of standardization.

Even the numbering system does little to clarify things. As the number of a hook decreases toward 1, the size increases. Thus, a size 2 hook is larger than a size 6. That changes once size 1 is reached. A /O is added after the number (1/0, 2/0, 3/0, 4/0, etc.). Now the size increases with the numbers. A 1/0 is larger than a 1, 3/0 larger than a 2/0, and so forth.

Along with some of the short-shanked tuna hooks, the O'Shaughnessy pattern ranks among the most popular for general salt water use. It's senseless to stock a supply of a dozen or more styles. A better approach suggests you find no more than six patterns and carry them in the appropriate sizes for your fishing. You may even get by with less if you limit the species you pursue.

The key to hook selection really centers on size and wire diameter. The smaller the size and the lighter the wire from which the hook is made, the better your chances of burying

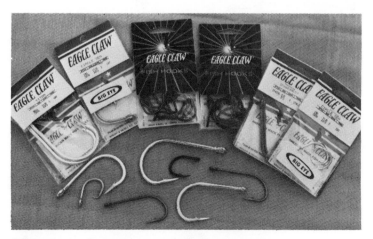

Select the hook that best compliments your tackle and type of fishing.

HOW TO SHARPEN A HOOK

SIDE CUT

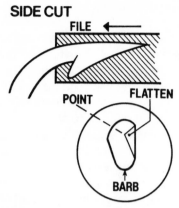

Used on new hooks out of the box, the SIDE CUT flattens one side, reducing wire diameter. With the point of the hook on top and the eye toward you, lay the sharpening tool against one side of the hook, keeping it parallel. Make several strokes toward the bend of the hook until that side is flattened. Don't flatten both sides.

DIAMOND

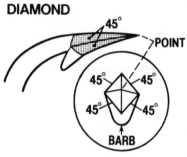

A properly formed DIAMOND produces four cutting edges plus a sharp point that many anglers consider the ultimate. It is nothing more than two Half-Diamonds back to back with one on top of the hook point and the second against the barb.

HALF DIAMOND

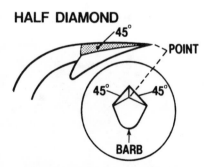

The HALF-DIAMOND ranks as the most popular method for sharpening hooks because it is effective and easy. Make a Standard Cut on one side of the point (opposite the barb) and a second Standard Cut on the other side. Done correctly, it produces a cutting edge on top and minor ones on either side.

TRIANGLE

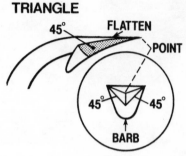

Triangulation develops three cutting edges, but it takes time to do. It's worth the effort where the rewards are important. Start by laying the sharpening tool at right angles to the top of the hook point. Hold the hook the same way you would in other methods. Flatten the top of the hook and then put a Half-Diamond Cut on the underside of the point against the barb, forming a TRIANGLE.

STANDARD CUT

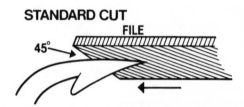

The STANDARD CUT is the basic stroke for most hook sharpening. With the point of the hook on top and the eye toward you, lay the tool against one side at a 45° angle. Stroking should be done from the point toward the bend. If you stroke from the bend toward the point, there may be a burr or nub on the point that must be removed.

SHORT BARB

Think of a barb as a wedge that hinders penetration. By reducing the height of the barb, it's easier to get a hook in a hard-mouthed fish. Both barbless and short barbed hooks hold surprisingly well and penetrate effectively.

SHORT POINT

Driving a hook point into the mouth of a fish may prove difficult on some species. Shortening the point and then resharpening it is one way to increase the odds with tarpon, billfish, and other animals with cinder block mouths.

he barb in the mouth of a fish. Obviously, you'll discover limitations. One cannot expect to hold a marlin with 50-pound tackle and a 1/0 light wire hook. If you happened to have a 12-pound outfit tethered to that same marlin, the 1/0 hook might be fine.

The basic rule lies in matching the hook to your tackle and to the species you intend to catch. Anglers everywhere have a tendency to use oversized hooks. For some reason, they insist that the larger, heavier hooks will hold more effectively. That thinking fails to consider how one should drive a husky hook into a tough mouth with light tackle and monofilament that stretches about 25 percent.

If you prefer to let the local tackle dealer choose the hooks for you, be sure to tell him the tackle you plan to use and the breaking strength of the line. You need smaller, lighter wire hooks with finer diameter monofilament regardless of the size fish you intend to catch.

By mashing the barb with a pair of pliers or shortening the distance between point and barb with a file, your success ratio of hookups will increase significantly. It's amazing how tenaciously a small, light hook can hold in a fish's mouth, even when you're tugging with every ounce of strength.

Rules have exceptions or at least caveats. When you're using live bait, you must consider the effect of the hook on the bait's swimming ability. Too large and heavy a hook will not allow the bait to perform properly. It has to be able to swim and send out distress vibrations.

For years, conservation-minded anglers urged fellow fishermen to use bronze hooks, arguing that they tended to rust out more quickly after a fish was released or if it broke off. The fact remains that it takes an inordinate amount of

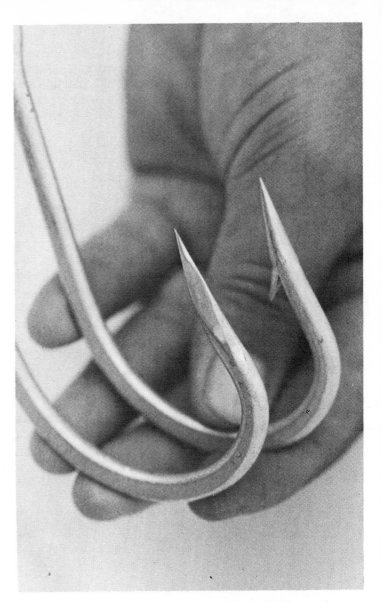

Sharpening a hook's outer point promotes a cutting action, requiring less pressure to set it.

and the hook drops out or the fish is able to work it free in some other manner. It's still the best policy to cut the leader and leave the hook when a fish is hooked deeply.

SWIVELS

Swivels prevent twist in fishing line caused by rotation of the bait or the lure. Engineers refer to them as primitive thrust bearings that handle a rotational force called torque, while dealing simultaneously with the load resulting from pulling something through the water. On the practical side, buy the best swivels you can find; it's cheap insurance against line twist and they may keep you from losing trophy fish.

As simple as a swivel appears, it really represents an attempt to counter some complex forces. Poor quality or inadequate engineering may produce failure because the linear load (straight pull) destroys the ability to swivel or turn.

You already know that you want fine diameter and small size in terminal tackle. The rule holds with swivels. Use the smallest that will do the job. In this instance, smaller swivels sometimes work better than larger ones for complicated reasons.

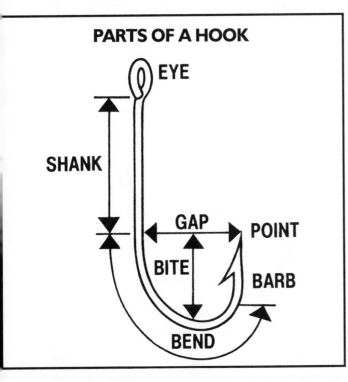

PARTS OF A HOOK

EYE

SHANK

GAP

POINT

BITE

BARB

BEND

time for any metal to rust if it stays under water and has little contact with air. If this weren't true, most of the relics from old ships discovered on the sea floor would have disintegrated years ago.

Eventually, fish do get rid of hooks. The hole enlarges

Swivel types include the twisted eye barrel, split eye barrel, bead chain, and ball bearing. The twisted eye is easy to spot. Look for the loop or eye to be formed by twisted wire. These represent the poorest quality you can find and are no longer made in the United States. They're imported in large numbers.

Split eye barrel swivels rank higher on the scale than the twisted eye. A piece of wire extends from the barrel and forms the loop or eye. Unlike the twisted eye, there are no twists in the wire. These are commonly used, but still lack quality.

Bead chain falls into the swivel category and does a relatively good job of reducing line twist. They're strong, flexible, and relatively inexpensive. You'll find them on trolling sinkers and other types of terminal rigs. If they have a shortcoming, it centers on their length. This type of swivel is longer than any of the others.

Ball bearing swivels sit at the top of the pile. Although some perform better than others, any ball bearing swivel is far superior to the other types. Rolling friction is much less than sliding friction. Originally, ball bearing swivels found a home on the offshore grounds for big game fishing. Now that they are made in an assortment of sizes including some that are very small, you can find the right ones for any assignment.

Bottom fishermen frequently rely on three-way swivels. Most are of the twisted eye variety, but some follow the split eye configuration. The three eyes or loops provided a place to attach the main line, the leader and hook, and a sinker. You'll find them in a variety of sizes. Again, choose the smallest ones that will do the job.

Snap swivels combine a swivel with a snap. They make it easy to change leaders. You merely open the snap, drop a loop previously tied in the end of the leader in the opening, and close the snap. You'll find several types of snaps and we'll let you decide which is best for your needs.

If you're having a problem with line twist (and it isn't being caused by cranking a spinning reel when the drag is slipping), try two small swivels instead of one big one. Where you place the swivels also makes a difference. At least one swivel must be attached to the main line and rest between it and any terminal tackle. Even with trolling sinkers and bead chain, it's a good idea to put a quality swivel between the sinker and the main line.

Bottom fishermen employ all types of spreaders and other attachments guaranteed to catch fish. We prefer to eliminate all this hardware and develop the smallest and simplest combinations. Knot systems often allow you to replace terminal hardware and achieve a more delicate and effective presentation.

Once you learn a few knots including the Bimini Twist, you have the option of creating rigs without swivels. In many instances, unknowing anglers use swivels as a means of connecting line and leader rather than knotting them together directly. The right knots create a 100 percent system; knots tied to swivel usually have less strength.

Removing line twist frequently proves difficult. If you have to do it, cut off all the terminal tackle including any swivels. Stream out all the twisted line behind a moving boat, put the rod in a holder, and drag the line around for awhile. That should remove the twist. If it doesn't, you're alternative

lies in replacing the line. Once that happens, you'll apprec ate the value of quality swivels.

WEIGHTED DOWN

Lead is relatively inexpensive, 11 times heavier tha water, and the primary material used in the molding sinkers. With few exceptions, the rule dictates that you u the lightest weight that will carry your offering to the botto or the desired depth. More weight is not necessarily bette particularly when you want a sinker to roll around and mov the bait across the bottom at a slow speed.

The weight of the sinker required works as a function line diameter. The lighter the line, the less weight you nee to achieve the same results in a given situation. If you're fis ing 12-pound test line and your partner spooled 17-poun your sinker should be lighter than his.

Sinkers are sold in every imaginable shape, but only handful will cover most angling assignments. Bank sinke lead the popularity parade because they seem to avoid fou ing on most bottoms. Although the bank sinker holds re sonably well, the pyramid has long been a favorite of su fishermen because it tends to dig in and grip, even in th turmoil of a crashing surf.

The dipsy style rolls around nicely over a relative smooth bottom, moving the bait over a wide area. Egg sinke

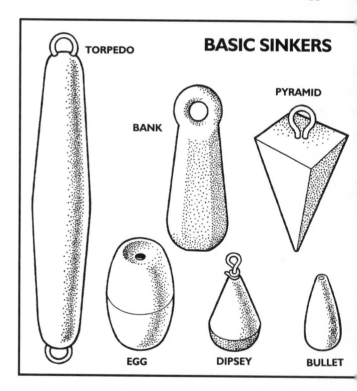

BASIC SINKERS

TORPEDO

BANK

PYRAMID

EGG

DIPSEY

BULLET

do a similar job and allow a fish to pull the line without de tecting the weight of the sinker.

The torpedo shape heads the list of trolling sinkers, bu some follow a banana shape. They have eyes on both end and many employ bead chain and a snap on at least one end Certain fishing situations require break away sinkers tha come loose once the fish is hooked. You can learn to mak your own with light, copper wire. On the West Coast, salmo anglers frequently rely on cannonball shapes that fall fre once the salmon takes the bait.

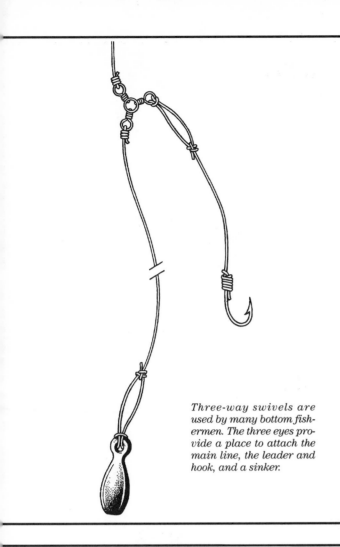

Three-way swivels are used by many bottom fishermen. The three eyes provide a place to attach the main line, the leader and hook, and a sinker.

Every tackle box should contain at least one package of split shots and rubber core sinkers. You might even add a few packages of bullet-shaped, worm weights. They have plenty of applications on the marine front. If you're rigging offshore lures, use small egg sinkers as a stop to keep the hook from shifting into the head of the lure.

Again, don't buy sinkers at random. Fishing with the correct shape and weight makes a major difference in the catch rate. Carry the styles and the weight ranges you use most frequently. And toss in some split shots, worm weights, and rubber cores for those special times when you need to add a little weight.

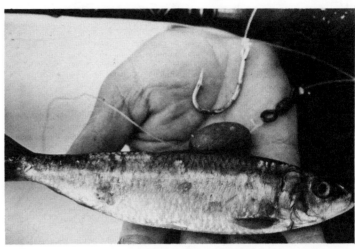

Swivels prevent twist in fishing lines. This leader system is connected to the Bimini twist with a barrel swivel. Note the sinker riding above it.

VENEZUELAN RIG

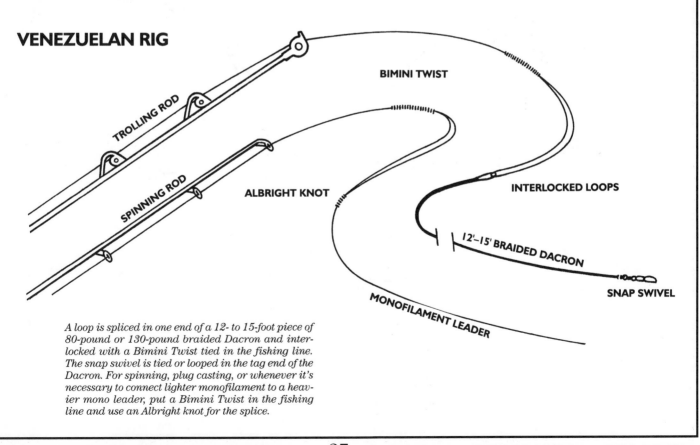

A loop is spliced in one end of a 12- to 15-foot piece of 80-pound or 130-pound braided Dacron and interlocked with a Bimini Twist tied in the fishing line. The snap swivel is tied or looped in the tag end of the Dacron. For spinning, plug casting, or whenever it's necessary to connect lighter monofilament to a heavier mono leader, put a Bimini Twist in the fishing line and use an Albright knot for the splice.

SURGEON'S KNOT

The Surgeon's Knot is a quick, effective, and strong way to tie two lines together of unequal diameters. It is excellent for attaching shock leaders.

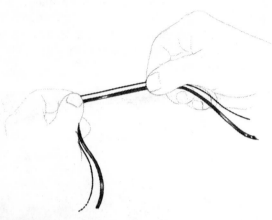

STEP 1
Lay the tag end of the main fishing line against the tag end of the heavier leader. Each tag end points in the opposite direction. Hold the lines together with the thumb and forefinger of both hands, leaving about a foot between the hands.

STEP 3
Bring the tag end of the fishing line and the standing part of the leader through the overhand knot (Step 2) a second time.

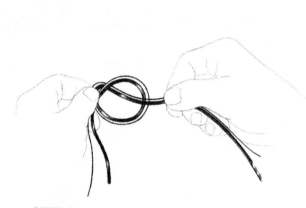

STEP 2
Make a simple overhand knot with both lines, remembering to keep them together at all times.

STEP 4
Moisten the double overhand knot. While holding both lines in each hand, start to pull your hands apart to tighten the knot. When the knot is as tight as you can make it, drop the two tag ends and pull on both standing parts.

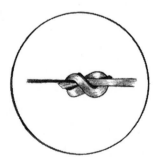

STEP 5
Trim the two tag ends and you are ready to fish. It's a quick method for attaching a leader.

DOUBLE SURGEON'S LOOP

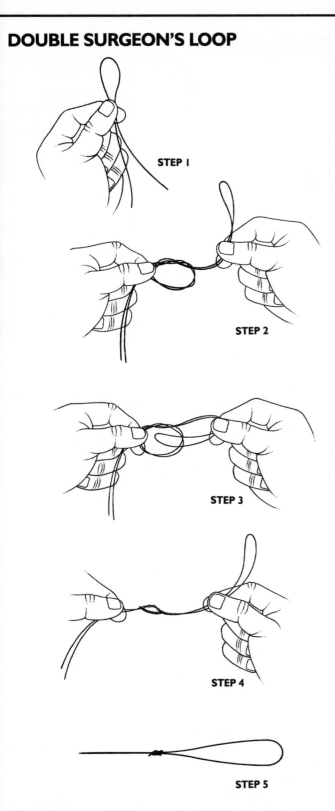

ALBRIGHT KNOT

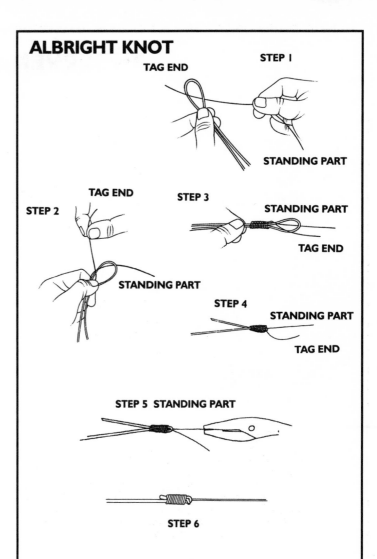

The Double Surgeon's loop is a quick and easy way to tie a loop in the end of a leader. STEP 1: Double the tag end of the line. STEP 2: Make a simple overhand knot in the double line. Hold the tag end and standing part of the line in your left hand and bring the loop around to insert it again in the overhand knot. STEP 3: Insert the end of the loop in the overhand knot. STEP 4: Hold both strands of the loop in your right hand and both the tag end and standing part in your left hand. Moisten the knot and pull your hands apart, tightening the knot. STEP 5: Trim off the tag end close to the knot and the finished product is a neat, quickly tied loop.

The Albright Knot is a useful knot for joining together monofilament lines of greatly unequal diameters and for joining monofilament and metallic traces. Illustrated here is connecting monofilament to monofilament. STEP 1: Bend a loop in the tag end of the heavier monofilament and hold the loop between the thumb and forefinger of your left hand. Insert the tag end of the lighter monofilament through the loop. The knot is now tied identically to the Albright connecting monofilament to wire. STEP 2: Slip the tag end of the lighter monofilament under your left thumb and pinch it tightly against the heavier strands of the loop. Wrap the first turn of the lighter monofilament over itself and continue wrapping toward the round end of the loop. You must take at least twelve turns with the lighter monofilament around all three strands. STEP 3: After you've completed at least twelve turns, insert the tag end of the lighter monofilament through the end of the loop. Remember that the monofilament must enter and leave the loop on the same side of the loop. STEP 4: With the thumb and forefinger of the left hand, slide the coils of lighter monofilament together and toward the end of the heavy monofilament loop, stopping within 1/8 inch of the end. STEP 5: Using pliers for a better grip, pull the tag end of the lighter monofilament tight. This must be done first or the coils will slip off the loop. Your left hand should still be holding both strands of the heavier monofilament. With your left hand still holding both the standing part and tag end of the heavier monofilament, pull on the standing part of the lighter monofilament. Then, pull the tag end of the monofilament a second time and the standing part of the monofilament once more. Now shift your left hand to only the standing part of the heavy monofilament (releasing the tag end of the heavy mono). Pull the standing part of the heavy mono and the standing part of the light mono. If the knot is going to fail, it should pull apart in your hands. STEP 6: Trim both tag ends closely.

THE SEVEN-STEP BIMINI

STEP 1

Start with about six feet of line and double the tag end back against the standing part to form a loop. Hold both the tag end and standing part firmly with the left hand, while you slip the four fingers of your right hand in the loop. Keep the loop fairly tight by separating your hands. Then, rotate your right hand twenty times in a clockwise direction, twisting one strand of line around the other.

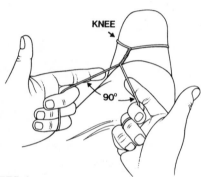

STEP 2

Prop your right foot on a tackle box, chair, cooler, etc. that will cause the knee to flex and bend. Slip the loop still held in your right hand over the bent knee. Keep the line tight so the twists cannot unravel. Separate the standing part of the line (left hand) from the tag end (right hand) so that they form a 90° angle. Pull the tag end and standing part toward you evenly, maintaining tension and a 90° angle. The twists will tighten and move toward the knee.

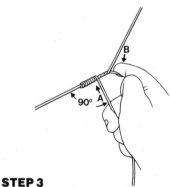

STEP 3

Once the twists are tight, shift the position of both hands to the right, retaining the 90° angle. The standing part is in line with the twists and the tag end is at right angles to them. As you pull on the standing part with your left hand, the tag end in your right hand will start to feed over the twists. Maintain moderate tension, but allow the line to feed (A). The forefinger of your right hand placed in the loop and pulled toward you will help the tag end to feed smoothly.

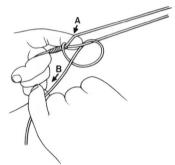

STEP 4

When the wraps over the twists reach the junction of the loop (which is still over your knee), hold them in place (A) by pushing against the twists with the forefinger of your left hand. Make a single half-hitch with the tag end around the right leg of the loop and pull the tag end (B) until the half-hitch seats. You no longer have to maintain tension and may remove the loop from your knee.

STEP 5

To finish the knot with a locking hitch, hold both legs of the loop together with your right hand or slip the loop over any projection. Lay the tag end against both legs, leaving enough slack underneath to form a semi-circle. Wrap the tag end around both legs of the loop five times, passing each turn inside the semi-circle. You are working back toward the twist. Moisten the wraps and pull the tag end slowly.

STEP 6

As you pull the tag end (arrow) slowly, the locking hitch continues to form. You may have to use the thumb and forefinger of your right hand to draw the wraps back as you tighten so that they don't jump over the knot.

STEP 7

Draw the locking hitch down as tightly as you can (use pliers if necessary) and trim the tag end close to the knot. You just tied a Bimini Twist.

igging natural baits is one of the true arts in sportfishing. This white marlin blasted a skipping ballyhoo.

earning to rig and fish natural baits is one of the true arts
sportfishing. The experienced angler knows how to study
e water and gamefish migrations, factoring these determi-
ations into his bait selection. He'll take into account the
ominent forage, how easy they are to procure for bait and
e average size of the gamefish he's interested in. This in-
rmation will help in choosing the most effective bait size,
ader type and rigging system.

There are numerous popular coastal baits, and even
ore methods of rigging them. There's no great secret in-
lved in mastering the technique just as long as you adhere
a few basic rules. The most important factor is to obtain
e freshest baits possible. Those that are fresh, or immedi-
ely brined and frozen after capture weather the strain of
onstant trolling. Baits inadequately handled quickly wash
t and tear easily on a strike. And don't overlook scent. A
esh bait is much more enticing, sometimes making the dif-
rence when a finicky fish appears in the spread.

Below are several highly effective ways of rigging
pular trolling baits. Learning them can be enjoyable
d profitable.

BALLYHOO:

The wire/pin rig is the most versatile ballyhoo arrangement. It's popular among offshore trollers where there's a
risk of a cut-off by toothy predators such as wahoo, kingfish
and barracuda. Providing a relatively light wire leader is used
(between 90 and 110-pound test), billfish rarely have a difficult time handling a bait. It's a good, all-around performer.

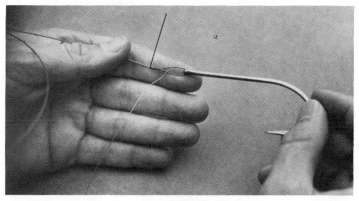

1.) Take 12-feet of stainless steel wire leader, forming a loop at one end with a Haywire twist/barrel wrap combination (this "loop" is attached to the trolling outfit's snap swivel). For medium and large baits, select an 8/0 or 9/0 long shank, needle eye hook (upgrading to an extra strength model and a larger size with 50-pound test tackle). Run the leader's tag end through the hook eye, forming a loop just large enough to prevent binding. Leave about two inches of the tag end exposed. Using thumb pressure, position the tag end upright and at a 180 degree angle from the hook's point. Attach a strand of soft rigging wire through the loop, firmly wrapping one end around the leader a few times.

2.) Take a ballyhoo and hold the hook alongside it to determine where the hook will ride once it's imbedded in the bait (you can expose the "bite" as much as you like by varying the distance the hook is threaded into the ballyhoo). Run the hook under the bait's gill plate, through the body cavity and out its underside, contorting the bait similar to threading a plastic bass worm onto a hook. Gently slide the hook back into the fish, positioning the leader's tag end just under the lower jaw.

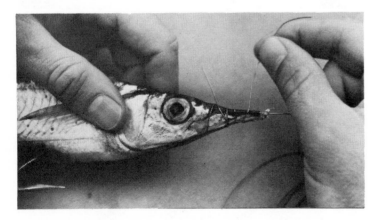

3.) Insert the tag through the lower and upper jaw, snap off about 3/4 of the beak, and take two firm wraps behind the tag with the rigging wire once you've made sure the leader is centered below the beak's base. Continue the tight wrap down the fish's beak, completing it with two wraps around the leader. Double back and clip any excess wire. You can dress up a ballyhoo by adding skirts, or give it more of a swimming-like appearance by inserting a barrel sinker onto the leader before securing the hook. The sinker should ride snugly under the bait's lower jaw.

THE MONOFILAMENT BALLYHOO:

Monofilament leaders are preferred on billfish, tuna an dolphin. A flexible leader increases a bait's action and offer little interference when a fish attempts to swallow it. For do phin, small tuna, sailfish and white marlin, an 80-pound tes leader is sufficient. Leaders testing around 300-pounds ar recommended when fishing large baits for blue marlin.

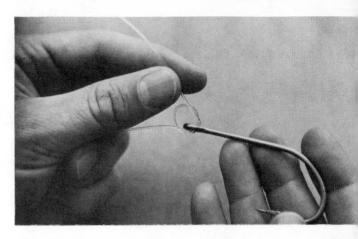

1.) Take 12-feet of monofilament and form an overhan loop knot. This will connect with the trolling outfit's sna swivel. Choose a semi-long shank, ring eye hook in a size be tween 7/0 and 9/0 (upgrade to a larger, extra strength mod el with 50-pound test gear). Slide two sleeves down the ta end, then insert the mono leader through the hook's ey twice (forming a circle loop).

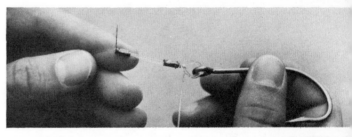

2.) Push the tag end through both sleeves (NOTE: th second sleeve simply serves as a spacer and adds depth s that the hook can be positioned farther back into a bait Crimp the sleeve closest to the connection. Before crimpin the second sleeve, leave two inches of the tag line exposed Fold back the tag end against the sleeve at a 180 degree an gle from the hook point. Run a strand of soft rigging wir through the hook loop, firmly wrapping one end around th leader a few times.

3.) Hold the hook alongside the ballyhoo to determine
where it will ride in the bait. Then, break off about 3/4 of its
beak. Run the hook under the gill plate, through the body cavity, and out its underside. Again, expose as much or as little
of the hook as you like by varying the distance it's threaded
into the ballyhoo. Using an ice pick or a hook point, bore a
small channel through the bait's lower and upper jaws. Run
the monofilament pin through this channel and fold back.
Secure the rig by firmly wrapping the soft wire strand twice
behind the pin and then down the beak and onto the leader.
Make sure the leader is centered below the lower beak.

THE WEEDLESS BALLYHOO:

This rig is used almost exclusively in dolphin fishing
when scattered weeds make trolling a real chore. Either a
monofilament or wire leader will work.

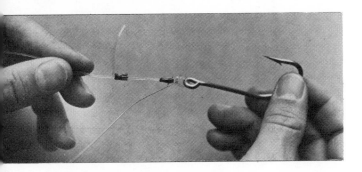

1.) Take the appropriate hook, place it in a vice-grip and
offset the point about five degrees to either side of the shank.
If you wish, bend the eye slightly upward. Run two sleeves
down the tag end of a 12-foot long monofilament leader before forming a circle loop around the hook. Run the tag end
through both sleeves (leave two inches exposed), making
sure it parallels the hook barb (reverse the hook). Crimp the
connection. Bend the mono pin against its sleeve and add a
strand of soft rigging wire to the "loop".

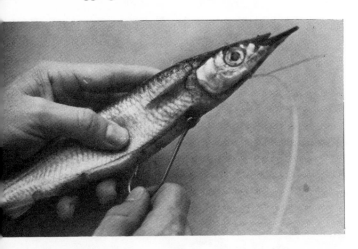

2.) Measure the rig alongside a ballyhoo to determine
where the hook will ride. Break off about 3/4 of the ballyhoo's beak. Next, run the hook through the gill plate, immediately exiting the body. Pull the entire hook through the
body cavity. Slightly contort the bait and insert the point back
into the belly. Straighten the ballyhoo, place the pin through
the lower and upper jaws (bore a small hole with a hook or

ice pick) and firmly wrap the soft wire twice behind the pin.
Finish the wrap by working it down the beak and onto the
leader. Make sure hook eye is placed back inside its cavity.

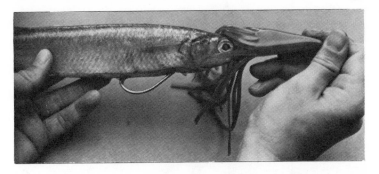

3.) Slip a plastic skirt down the leader and over the bait's
head, which will deflect weeds in addition to prolonging its
durability. Form an overhand loop knot in the leader for the
trolling outfit's snap swivel.

TESTING YOUR BALLYHOO

A well tuned ballyhoo is one where the strain of trolling
is absorbed by the bait's head, not the hook. A simple test requires holding the ballyhoo with one hand and pulling on the
leader with the other. If the hook doesn't respond to the tension, chances are it'll troll well. A spinning bait often indicates that either the rigging wire isn't wrapped tightly around
the bait's beak, or the hook is pulling against the body cavity. In the latter case, a slight incision in the cavity should relieve the binding.

MULLET

Mullet is a cherished bait among offshore enthusiasts.
They're readily available, durable, flashy, and swim surprisingly well when rigged properly. Jumbo baits bettering two
pounds are sought for trophy marlin. The smaller billfishes
and most pelagics respond more favorably to mullet weighing nearly eight-ounces. The streamlined silver mullet is preferred for trolling over the blunt-headed black mullet. Both
wire and monofilament leaders are used.

SWIMMING MULLET

1.) Set aside a 12-foot wire leader with a loop in one end
(Haywire twist). Use at least 15-feet for marlin. Insert a
deboner (a tool that cores out backbones of medium to large

baitfish) under a gill plate, moving it upward and onto the front of the backbone and then down its entire length with a slow, steady twisting motion. Several twists at a slight angle should detach the backbone near the tail. Remove the deboner and expel its contents with the push rod. If a deboner isn't available, remove the backbone by making long incisions along both sides of the dorsal fin. Sew the cavity closed with dental floss or waxed thread, making sure no large openings exist to catch water.

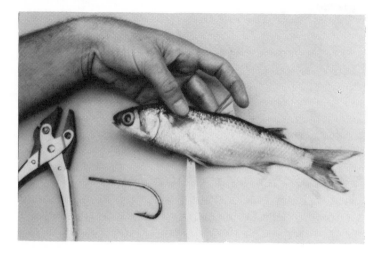

2.) Make an incision in the belly for the hook eye to penetrate, pushing the shank forward until the eye rests inside the mullet's mouth.

3.) Add an egg sinker to the leader before running it through the lower jaw, hook eye, and out the head (use an ice pick to bore your hole). Position the weight under or just forward of the lower jaw, holding it firmly in place with a Haywire twist/barrel wrap combination. Although not a necessity, dental floss can be used to "wire" the gill plates shut.

SKIPPING MULLET
Follow the procedures listed above but replace the weight with a tight Haywire twist.

SOME WORDS ON MULLET
The proper hook and leader material should be selected according to bait size and tackle. For example, a number 9 or 10 leader wire and a 9/0 long shank, needle-eye hook in eight-ounce class baits are sufficient for tackle approaching 50-pound test. The ideal weight for a swimming bait depends on the mullet's size, sea conditions and boat speed. A good ru[le] of thumb is to pair baits approaching 10-inches in leng[th] with weights close to one-ounce. Baits as long as 12-inch[es] swim best with as much as three-ounces of weight. The s[e]cret is to get the job done with the least amount of weigh[t].

Monofilament leaders also increase a mullet's actio[n.] Substitute the needle eyes for ring eye hooks and crimp th[e] connections. With the exception of blue marlin, which r[e]quire monofilament in the 300-pound test range, 80 and 10[0] pound class leaders will handle most non-toothy pelagic[s.]

STRIP BAITS
One of the deadliest and simplest offerings to rig is th[e] strip bait. Created from the firm bellies and mid-sections [of] fish such as bonito, dolphin, tuna and barracuda, these bit[e]size imitations can withstand the rigors of offshore trollin[g] amazingly well and have decked just about all pelagics.

1.) Carve a strip from a fish's belly, trimming it to a to[r]pedo-like shape by rounding or blunting the head and strea[m]lining the body to a point at the tail. You can split the tail f[or] additional pulsating actions (NOTE: troll the bait with th[e] meat's grain to prevent premature washout).

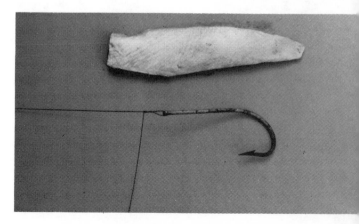

2.) Using the standard ballyhoo pin rig, align it so tha[t] the tag end is just inside and above the strip bait's leadin[g] edge.

3.) Insert the tag end and hook, respectively, through the strip. Check for binding.

4.) Sharply bend the tag end forward before wrapping it at least four times around the leader, folding back the exposed portion to prevent it from snagging debris. This setup enables a bait to be replaced in short order by simply unwinding the lead wrap and securing a fresh strip. Feathers and skirts add extra appeal.

SOME THOUGHTS ON STRIP BAITS

Trying to locate tackle shops or marinas that stock strip baits can become a never ending assignment. Captains often maintain their own supply by carving baits from the day's carcasses. Place the strips into a large jar, layering them with kosher salt. Cover the jar and set aside until they're needed. The salt will draw out moisture and preserve the baits. Make sure to trim the baits before salting and vary their sizes.

TROLLING SQUID

A squid is the premier trolling bait for marlin, dolphin and tunas. Although a little trickier to rig than most baits, they can endure hours of trolling, have an enticing surface action and contain a powerful scent. Furthermore, the squid is a natural forage of most offshore species since they inhabit oceans world-wide.

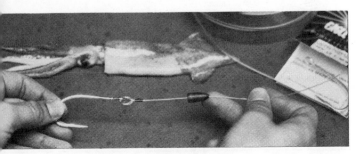

1.) Crimp a 9/0 ring-eye hook onto the end of a 12-foot long, 80-pound test monofilament leader. Trim the tag end. Next, slide a small barrel sinker down the leader. Measure the rig against a squid of about 10-inches in length (NOTE: The hook point should ride approximately between the eyes, if not closer to the mantle). Once you mark where the hook will lay, slide the sinker up to where it will abut the inside mantle, tying it in place with a soft wire wrap (you can also compress the sinker with a hammer, though take care not to damage the leader).

2.) Thread the hook into the squid's head, beginning at the juncture of the mantle and working down toward the eyes. Leave enough "bite" for the hook to be effective. Next, slide the leader inside the mantle and out the opposite end (NOTE: You may have to snip or bore a very small opening for leader access, perhaps using a rigging needle to "snake" it through).

3.) Once the sinker is snug against the mantle, check for any binding at the hook (the strain should be placed on the sinker/mantle, not the hook). Next, using either waxed line or sewing thread, sew the leader to the mantle (to close any openings that may catch water) just in front of and behind the sinker. Stitch the mantle and head together and also the hook shank to the head for added support. You may also want a stitch midway down the mantle. Form an overhand loop knot on the leader for the fishing line's snap swivel and you're in business.

BRINING BAITS

The secret to maintaining fresh baits is knowing how to create and manage a good brine. You'll need a cooler, plenty of ice, plastic bags (those from the ice will suffice) and a box of Kosher salt (iodized table salt will do in a pinch). In addition to keeping the brine temperatures just above freezing, salt will draw out moisture and toughen a bait.

Spread a thin layer of ice on the bottom of a cooler, dusting liberally with salt. Lay the empty ice bag over a section of the ice. Arrange several baits so their bodies lay on the ice and their leaders over the plastic bag. Place another bag over the leaders followed by another layer of ice and salt. Alternate sides when stacking baits and continue the procedure until full. Dust heavily with salt.

The melting ice and salt forms a briny slush that preserves baits for several days. Check the cooler daily, draining excess water and adding ice and salt. As you head offshore remove your starter baits and soak them in a bucket of sea water to loosen them up. The plastic bags should facilitate their removal since they protect the leaders from clinging to the ice.

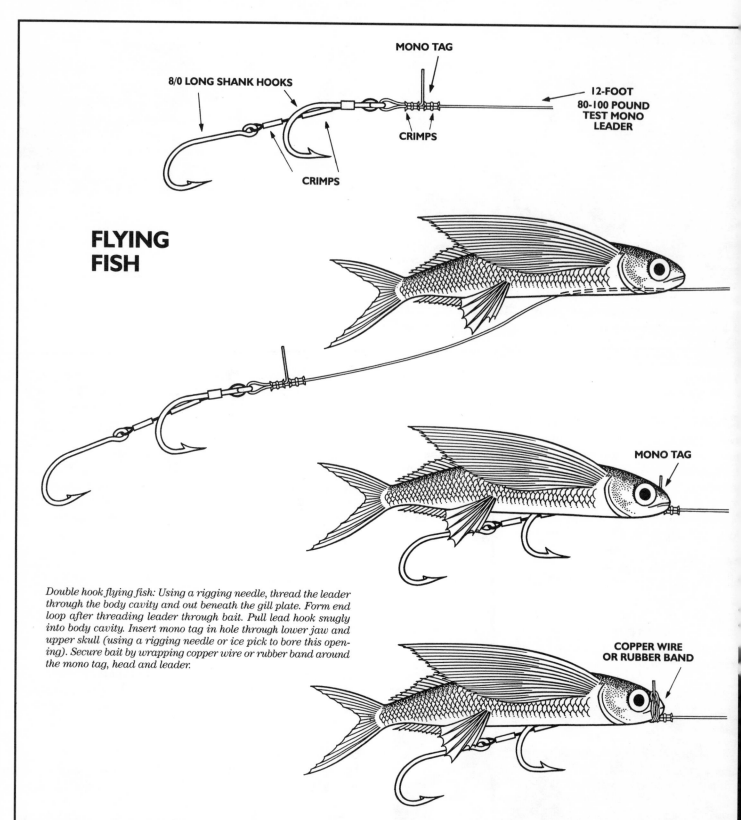

FLYING FISH

Double hook flying fish: Using a rigging needle, thread the leader through the body cavity and out beneath the gill plate. Form end loop after threading leader through bait. Pull lead hook snugly into body cavity. Insert mono tag in hole through lower jaw and upper skull (using a rigging needle or ice pick to bore this opening). Secure bait by wrapping copper wire or rubber band around the mono tag, head and leader.

8 AS THE TIDE TURNS

Tides and tidal currents play a significant role in where fish will be and when they will be there. By definition, tide is the vertical rise and fall of the water, while current represents horizontal movement. The distinction proves important. Anglers instinctively monitor the current as an indicator of a rising or falling tide. In some locations, the direction of the

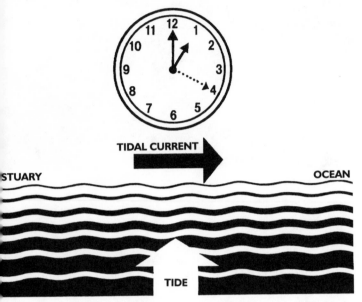

Tide is the vertical rise and fall of the water; current the horizontal flow. In some areas the current lags behind the change of tide. It might still be flowing seaward when the tide begins to rise.

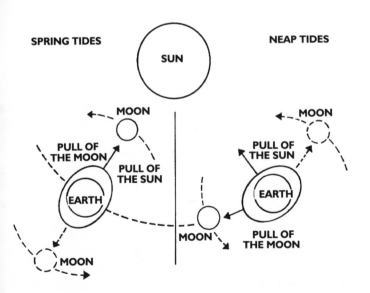

The gravitational pull of the moon and, to a lesser degree, the sun affect the tides. When they are in alignment, spring tides, characterized by higher highs, lower lows and stronger currents, occur. Neap tides take place when the moon is at right angles to the earth and not in line with the sun. Currents are weaker and tides have a smaller range.

current flow may lag the change of tide by as much as several hours. It may appear, for example, that the tide continues to fall when it has actually started to flood.

Most places report two high tides and two low tides daily known as semi-diurnal tides. Usually, one of the high tides produces a greater rise than the other, while one low tide may be a bit lower. Since the moon has a more pronounced effect on the tides than the sun, tides follow the lunar day which is about 50 minutes longer than the solar day. Tomorrow, the tides will be 50 minutes later than they were today.

Wind direction and changes in barometric pressure affect sea level and the amount of water on a given tide. Onshore winds and/or lower barometric pressure create higher tides than predicted. If the wind blows offshore or barometric pressure remains high, the water level is frequently lower.

Researchers report that the water level (tide) remains stationary for only an instant (called stand of the tide), although the transfer of water just prior to and immediately following the stand may not be perceptible. Slack water actually refers to the current, denoting the point at which current speed is near zero.

Current is seldom uniform. It starts slowly, builds to a peak, and then tapers off gradually. The greater the range between high and low tide, the stronger the current will be in both directions. If a large body of water drains and floods through a narrow neck, current velocity will increase dramatically. Tide also floods and ebbs at varying rates with the peak somewhere in the middle.

The gravitational pull of the moon and, to a lesser degree, the sun affect both tide and current. When the sun and moon are in alignment (new moon and full moon), the tides are called spring tides. Simply by looking at the moon, you can tell when there are spring tides or neap tides anywhere in the world.

Spring tides have higher highs, lower lows, and stronger currents because more water must be transferred in the same amount of time. Neap tides occur during the quarter moons when the sun and moon are at right angles. A lower tidal range and weaker currents characterize this phase.

Within a given area, the time of the tide for specific spots varies. It could be earlier or later than the predicted tide in the tables. Local knowledge and experience will help you to know how much the time of the actual tide differs from the tables for the sectors you intend to fish. Corrections are frequently published for the more popular places.

Old time mariners relied on the moon to determine when the tide would be flooding and when it might fall. If the moon (regardless of phase) is rising, the tide is coming in. A waning moon signals outgoing water.

Another rule of thumb worth remembering centers on the two-week cycle. If you fished today and high water occurred around noon, you can count on finding low water at noon one week from today. It takes two weeks for conditions to repeat.

Once you begin to understand where fish will be on a particular stage of the tide, picking the right spots becomes much easier.

GOING WITH THE FLOW

From a practical standpoint, gamefish respond to tidal stage and current flow. Being able to detect the precise direction of currents in a given area may increase your catch. Water seldom moves directly east or west along a coast. Even on shallow flats shouldering the sea, current sometimes moves obliquely across the bottom and seaward through the channels.

By carefully studying a current, you should be able to isolate areas where dead spots or eddies occur. Look for holes and depressions in the bottom that allow fish to avoid the force of the main flow. Sometimes, the edges produce zones of reduced flow where a fish could hold without exerting as much energy.

Fish instinctively use tides and currents to their advantage. They boast the ability to detect minor changes in water level and always know the direction of flow. Any fish that remains stationary in the water faces into the current. Note that the key word is current and not tide. A critter holding in a back eddy, for example, may be facing the opposite direction from its schoolmates a few feet away in the main flow.

Predators take up stations where they can intercept the food supply. Schools of forage species go with the flow rather than sap their energy and struggle against the current. Aggressive heavyweights may use their broad tails to chase hapless bait in tidal rips and in areas where the current is strong. Others hold just on the edges or behind some form of structure, darting out to grab a passing meal.

Cruising predators frequently work into the tide, expecting to bump into their prey going the other way. The sense of smell plays a role in this situation, because current carries the smell track. If you're downwind from an animal, it has difficulty picking up the scent. A natural bait down tide from a fish poses the same problem.

A bait or lure cast upcurrent and retrieved with the flow or across it has a better chance of success. Fish are facing in that direction and have a better chance to see or smell it. Besides, it looks more natural. They expect their food to come from that direction. Whenever you fish, always be aware of currents so that you can use them to your advantage.

WORKING THE TIDES

Experts talk about tides and currents in terms of stages. They recognize that water movement follows a progressive path, creating windows of opportunity. Fish continuously adjust to the various stages. Seldom will you find a feeding fish in the same place through an entire tide. Even if it doesn't roam far, count on that critter to fine tune its position to maximize comfort and locate food.

Tides play a major role in determining where fish will be and when they'll be there.

Trolling enthusiasts often drag baits from shallow to deep since there's a good chance that gamefish will be patrolling these edges.

Fishing an area on an outgoing tide where a relatively shallow shelf drops off into deep water may do the trick. Bait will be carried from the sanctuary of the shallows to the deep where gamefish are lurking.

Currents stimulate bait movements. Find a strong edge or area containing bait and your quarry shouldn't be far behind.

Catching fish centers on putting the puzzle pieces together. Once you begin to understand where fish will be on a particular stage of the tide, picking the right spots becomes much easier. Professional guides make a living based on this type of knowledge. Newcomers marvel at the mystery when a guide casually announces that fish will be in a certain area 20 minutes from now and it actually happens. He simply knows the tide and how the fish react to the various stages.

Let's put this into perspective with some practical examples. Picture an area where a relatively shallow shelf drops off into deep water. You would probably want to fish this on an outgoing tide when the current has built to a reasonable flow. Bait would be carried from the sanctuary of the shallows to the hazardous murkiness of the deep where gamefish are surely waiting to pick off an easy meal.

If you're trolling, think about dragging baits from shallo to deep, since this is the direction from which fish expe their food to come. Should that fail, try a zigzag course alo the edge. Working from deep to shallow ranks as the thi choice. Study the area carefully. You're looking for plac where the major flow of water would normally carry ba

Flooding water invariably produces better results alo rocky, coastal shorelines. The water may be deep enough hold your quarry on low water, but fishing usually turns o better on an incoming tide.

Overhanging trees along a shore create another pro lem. A rising tide pushes water back under the branches ar among the root system. Baitfish instinctively seek a have there and husky predators often follow. Nothing is more fru trating than to hear the repeated showering of bait und the trees, knowing that you can't get a bait or lure to tl fish.

Tide becomes the catalyst for flats fishermen. The quarry invades the thin water with the flood tide and fal back once the tide starts to ebb. Learning a flat demands p tience and experience. Some produce better results on ou going water, while others come to life with the push of tl flood. If you don't know a flat, start your investigation at lo tide and follow the incoming water. Fish often trade bac and forth along the edge, waiting for the rise.

Depending on the area, your quarry may put in an aj pearance when the tide starts to flood, at any stage up l high tide, or during a phase of the fall. You have to be ther to learn when it is going to happen.

About the time one thinks he has figured out the bas tidal patterns, moon phases enter the picture. During nea tides, fish may work flats in certain patterns, falling back tl way they came when the water level drops. On spring tide these same fish will roam farther over the flat because ther is more water and they may exit via a totally different route Some sectors may only hold fish on spring tides and be ba ren the rest of the time. Neap tide spots may lose fish durin spring tides. It's a learning process and a tough one.

A greater push of water on some tropical flats drive species such as bonefish into the mangroves where you can get to them. There are places that are only fishable whe the tide is high early in the morning. This gives you falling wi ter during the morning and the first of the rise in the afte noon. Otherwise, the fishing window becomes greatly re duced. Too much water on a flat (spring tides) may make difficult to see fish.

It's difficult to fathom the effect of tides on the offshor grounds, but a correlation does exist. We've seen fishing fo marlin improve dramatically on falling water in depths ove 1,000 feet. Possibly, the moving water set up favorable cu rents or fish responded to an inner reckoning with the tid clock.

Certainly if you are fishing a reefline, work the offshor side on an outgoing tide. Any water movement will push ba seaward. Inlets, river mouths, funnel necks, and othe drainage areas also seem to produce better results on fallin water. No one has ever explained the connection satisfacto rily between fish and tides in blue water, but it's worth mor itoring. Many of us can only guess why it happens, but the re lationship still proves valuable.

MOON PHASES

An itinerant philospher once mused in passing that the best time to fish is when you are there. The pressures of uttering other profound statements kept him from advancing the corollary that you catch more fish if you happen to be there at the right time.

Serious anglers frequently talk about the effect of moon phases on fishing. Most of the theories evolve through local observations and often prove to be surprisingly accurate. If you fish for blue marlin in St. Thomas, Virgin Islands during the three days leading up to the full moon in July and August, you can almost be guaranteed a fish.

Travel to La Guaira, Venezuela for the white marlin spectacular in September or October and skippers insist that fishing slows around the full moon. They prefer the new moon. Notice that most of the differences center on full moon versus new moon. Part of the problem certainly involves the amount of light. The thinking is that many gamefish feed at night when there is significant brightness. Perhaps the stronger gravitational pull during the periods of new and full moon somehow affect these animals.

If you keep a fishing log (and you should), be sure to note factors such as moon phase along with precise tidal data. Eventually, you might start to unravel some of the patterns that apply to the waters you fish regularly. We often make it a point to ask others what their experience has been regarding moon phases and fish activity. Those who have

Certain fish feed more aggressively during specific moon phases. Would this plump snapper have consumed a bait during a full moon?

monitored this aspect usually have positive opinions and they help to stimulate our thinking.

TIDES, MOONS, AND TRAVEL

The anticipation of a fishing vacation often clouds common sense, particularly when it involves a trip to a dream location for exotic species. No matter where in the world you pursue gamefish, the same factors affect the fishing as they do back home. Ignore them and you court disappointment and frustration.

The most obvious centers on seasons. Even when a particular species swims in local waters year around, you'll discover that some months are much better than others. People travelling to warm climates assume they are journeying to the land of perpetual summer where the popular species will certainly be abundant anytime. That's not the case. You want to be there when a major run is in progress and that involves timing. Taking a chance on scoring in the off-season doesn't make sense.

Calculate tides carefully. When there are spring tides in New York, you can count on finding spring tides in Hong Kong. These will occur a few days before and a couple of days after the full and new moons. Determining whether the tides will be spring or neap when you arrive at your destination merely solves the first part of the equation. You really want to know the time of the tides as well. If it is important to fish incoming water, for example, you don't want a low tide that occurs at 2:00 p.m. That doesn't leave much time before nightfall to work the incoming.

The National Oceanic and Atmospheric Administration (NOAA) publishes annually Tide Tables for East Coast of North and South America. A companion volume covers the west coast. If you can talk directly to the guide or to the resort manager when making reservations, you should be able to get answers to questions on tides. Most folks simply don't ask these vital questions. They're too interested asking how many fish they'll catch each day or what the weather will be. Make certain you know the ideal tide pattern and when it will occur. If you have flexibility in your scheduling, match your itinerary to take advantage of the best possible conditions.

Once you sort out the tides, bring up the topic of moon phase. Find out if the local specialist can recommend the best moon phase or if he will at least issue a caveat about certain ones. Basically, you want to know whether a full moon has a positive or negative effect on the fish. That's the primary question if you only have time for one.

A seasoned charter skipper who has taken sportfishing boats across the seas of the world told us that he tries to avoid starting a journey during the period leading up to the full moon. According to his observations, storms and rough seas frequently sweep through an area on this moon phase. Given a choice, he will leave port two or three days after the full moon and claims the sailing is much smoother.

No matter where you fish or the species you seek, studying the tides, tidal currents, and moon phases should become an ongoing process. These factors hold the key to finding fish on both the inshore and the offshore grounds. Your quarry responds to tides and uses them to its advantage. You should, too.

Whether fished off a downrigger, a kite, or simply slow-trolled, a live bait is devastating on gamefish. That's a 66-pound kingfish; the victim of a "livie."

THE TRIPLE THREAT

DOWNRIGGERS, WIRE LINES AND KITES

Salt water fishing conditions never stay the same. While an angler periodically uncovers fish feeding at or near the surface, he realizes that such a find may be short lived and he'd better take quick advantage of it. When the action cools or waters seem void of life, far too many anglers continue plying traditional surface techniques hoping to stumble into fish. The fact is, confining one's techniques solely to the surface limits his ability to a mere ten-percent of the water column.

Think about it. If fish have retreated into the depths, what does it take to draw them up? Fish respond to specific temperatures that dictate their migrations, spawning, feeding habits and aggressiveness. If surface layers become intolerable for both bait and fish, or if there's an abundance of bait at mid and lower depths, chances of luring a fish back on top are remote. Those who catch fish consistently rely on techniques that penetrate a major portion of the water column, simultaneously taking advantage of the surface, mid-depth and lower ranges. If one zone seems "hot", another bait or two is adjusted to the activity.

Jigging is a simple and effective means of probing the depths, as are planers and trolling weights. However, the following instruments specialize in presenting baits within the water column. With a little insight and imagination, you can apply them to your fishing with good results.

Downriggers have opened up incredible fish-catching avenues for salt water anglers. They offer precise bait positioning and the option of using light-tackle since there's no cumbersome weight to deal with after the strike. You can troll, still drift, bottom fish and even chum with the versatile instrument.

DOWNRIGGERS:

Once regarded primarily as a fresh water tool to take a bait down in deep lakes and rivers, the downrigger is now an established option for salt water anglers. Although far from reaching its potential, the unique instrument has opened new doors in marine fishing and continues to increase the ability of those who consistently run them. Marketed as a trolling aid, incorporating captains find them just as effective when drifting and still fishing and even in teasing fish into baiting range.

The advantages of a downrigger are that depth can be controlled precisely and it's compatible with light tackle: a fishing line, held by a clip on the cable or weight, is released on a strike leaving an angler free of any cumbersome weights when playing a fish. Comprised of a revolving spool packed with stainless steel cable that's fed through a boom (arm), a lead ball, and a swivel base, a downrigger even displays its depth on a line counter.

Choosing one hinges on the type of fish it's intended for and budget. A simple, manual downrigger spooled with one hundred feet of cable is fine for inshore and most offshore applications. Prices vary from under $100 for a "bare-bones" version to around $300 for a heavy duty "work-horse" model with extra line capacity. And then there are the electric versions that automatically retrieve their clip after a strike and deploy a new bait at the exact depth, vary a bait's depth in ten foot increments at programmed intervals and even take sub-surface water temperatures. Prices range between $300 and $1,200, depending upon the features.

Most downriggers come with their own release clips, either on the cable or lead weight. However, a proven arrangement in both trolling and drifting situations consists of a snap swivel crimped at both ends of a six inch stretch of 300-pound-test monofilament, which the release clip rides on. The lead ball attaches to the bottom snap, whereas the opposite side attaches to the barrel swivel on the downrigger's cable. The release clip rides between a pair of small lead sinkers or plastic beads that'll prevent the crimps from hindering its freedom. The monofilament and swivels eliminate twist. A quality release clip enables you to precisely adjust its tension. You'll need an ultra light setting to lessen the resistance a fish feels when it takes a live bait (if a drop-back is desired), or a firm adjustment that imbeds the hook(s) of a swimming plug, spoon or other lure before the fishing line and clip part.

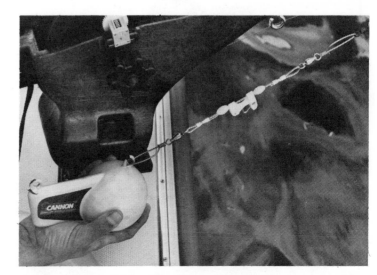

An outrigger or fishing kite clip on 300-pound-test mono with a swivel on either end is a neat and efficient above-the-weight downrigger arrangement.

THE PAY OUT

Deploying a downrigger is simple. Pay out the baits as if you're setting a trolling spread, and engage the reel drags. Form a loop in the fishing line intended for the downrigger by twisting it several times with your fingers. Place the loop into the release clip and adjust the setting. Slowly back-off the drags of the fishing reel and downrigger so both lines pay out very slowly (remember, Very Slowly: you're dealing with a substantial weight). At the desired depth, engage the downrigger's drag first, then adjust the fishing outfit's strike setting. Slowly wind line until the tip of the fishing rod bends, which springs back on a strike.

A "loop" in the fishing line locks it in place. If line is tethered through the downrigger clip similar to an outrigger, the pressure of the water meeting the line as the boat moves forward forms a belly. The expansion will continue, eventually drawing the bait to its release pin.

Scope in the downrigger cable develops as trolling speeds increase, reducing its accuracy. To hold a precise depth, anglers must compensate for this factor by paying out more cable. Exactly how much depends on trolling speed and sea conditions. However, downrigger authorities recommend doubling the amount of cable to reach a specific depth at speeds between five and ten knots. For example, keeping a bait at a depth of 50-feet at an eight knot trolling speed requires approximately 100-feet of downrigger cable. Anglers "bottom hugging" (fishing right above structure) mustn't forget about that extra cable after a hook-up, which needs to be retrieved before the boat is slipped into neutral to keep the lead weight from snagging bottom. Fortunately, downriggers have forgiving drags (when not locked down) that can prevent a boom from buckling if the unthinkable occurs. The doubling-the-depth formula is eliminated when drifting or slow trolling.

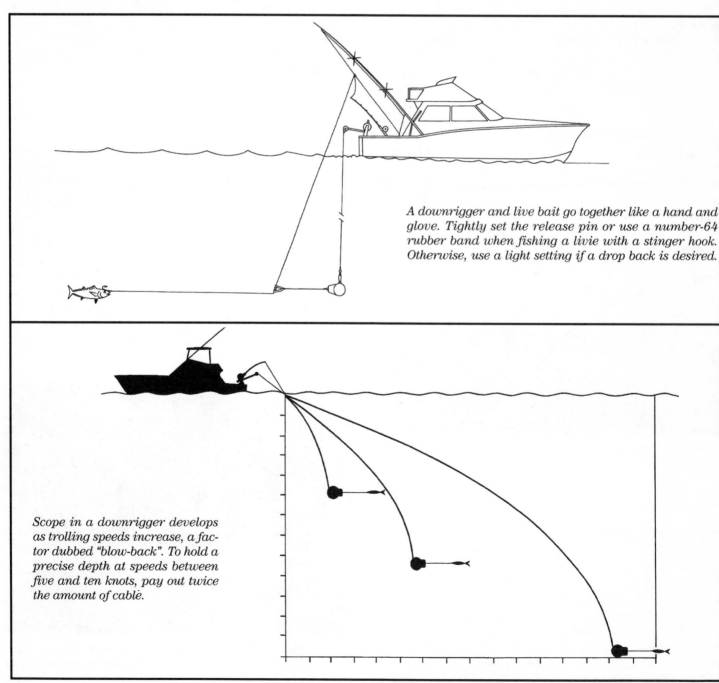

A downrigger and live bait go together like a hand and glove. Tightly set the release pin or use a number-64 rubber band when fishing a livie with a stinger hook. Otherwise, use a light setting if a drop back is desired.

Scope in a downrigger develops as trolling speeds increase, a factor dubbed "blow-back". To hold a precise depth at speeds between five and ten knots, pay out twice the amount of cable.

THE BEST BAIT

The golden rule about selecting a downrigger bait is that there are no rules. Whatever baits you're accustomed to trolling work just fine, although spoons and swimming plugs are strong favorites. Multiple baits can be fished off a single downrigger by using a "stacker" clip, a six inch plastic or metallic strand with compression clips at each end. After the main downrigger bait is headed down, attach one end of a stacker clip to the cable in a clothespin-like fashion, and the opposite end to the second fishing line. Continue lowering the cable until both baits are well below the surface. The stacker clip removes easily when you're checking on the deep bait and fits conveniently into any tackle box. It's a worthwhile addition.

trolling spoon fools plenty of fish. It's just as versatile offshore as it is inshore.

A downrigger bait is even more vulnerable in conjunction with a teaser. A large, hook-less trolling lure attached to the weight by three feet of heavy monofilament will wobble and dart behind it. Vibrations and actions emitted from the teaser just may attract fish and lure them to the loaded bait. One downrigger-style teaser that's netting results is a chrome dodger or hook-less trolling spoon that even reflects light. A hook-less chugger or darter-type plug is another great teaser and the offshore angler can go as far as running a squid daisy chain behind the weight. Despite taking their share of "shots" from fish, teasers add another dimension to downrigger fishing by building an attractive underwater spread.

JACK OF ALL TRADES

Downriggers are best associated with trolling, but they execute a number of specialty techniques. Captains chumming for yellowtail over the reefs and wrecks of southern Florida know the obstacles strong currents pose. Incorporating captains have succeeded in filtering chum through productive lairs by simply attaching a chum bag to the downrigger's weight, complete with a loaded bait dangling enticingly several feet above and behind it. Regardless of current, chum disperses through the targeted areas attracting bait and yellowtail. When a fish is hooked up, the downrigger is retrieved, re-loaded and sent back down. What's more, many a large grouper and mutton snapper have been tolled in by this technique, where scent, bait gatherings and activity lure them from their "holes". It's a deadly method that works on most bottom species.

Live baiters use downriggers to penetrate productive depths. In a still-drifting situation a live bait is tested at middepth and bottom ranges, whereas the remainder of the spread is at or just below the surface. With hearty baits such as menhaden, mullet and blue runners, hook a downrigger-bound one just above the anal fin. The pressure of the weight and tackle will inhibit its forward motion and the amount of water filtering through the gills. The oxygen restriction forces the bait to continuously swim from the pressure to maintain the flow, thus keeping it away from the downrigger weight and boat. Hooking a bait in front of the dorsal or through a lip may work the opposite, where it will swim toward the weight to alleviate the resistance and hang up in the downrigger cable.

Power drifting just up-current of structure is a specialized approach to fish a live bait on the threshold of a wreck or ledge. When a fish takes the bait, the boat is throttled forward to force it away from the lair. Probing the down-current side of structure is a matter of holding right over that edge and adjusting for the depth (paying close attention to a fishfinder for any deviation), or still drifting directly over the target and lowering the downrigger once the fishfinder indicates you've cleared it. In both cases, motor with the current off the structure to keep a hooked fish from reaching it.

A typical live-bait shotgun approach; baits are fished from a fishing kite, free-drifted near the surface and staggered in the depths on a downrigger.

WIRE LINE:

Anyone who has regularly chartered a boat throughout the years has to remember hooking a fish on a wire-line outfit and the extra effort and elbow grease it took to land it. As awkward as wire-line seems, it's too valuable of a tool to neglect.

Similar to a downrigger, it positions a bait below the surface. Unlike the downrigger, there's no eliminating the weight and precisely targeting a certain depth is contingent on factoring boat speed and the amount of line paid out. However, a wire line outfit complements most trolling spreads (downrigger included) and is equally effective probing the bottom as it is riding just beneath the surface. Although deadly effective in all waters, they're used primarily offshore in the southern and Gulf of Mexico states on pelagics like kingfish and wahoo, and for groupers, snappers and amberjack when dragged near bottom. In the Northeast they religiously take bluefish and striped bass. Some advocates even believe the vibrations emitted by the line attract fish.

WHAT IT'S MADE OF

Monel wire, a popular core, is an alloy of nickel, copper, iron, manganese, silicon and carbon. Compared to single strand stainless steel it's very soft, conforms well and is impervious to pitting and splintering. It's the weight of these solid core fishing lines and a trolling sinker that take baits down. A conventional 4/0 reel is suitable for most species, although 6/0s are common for large offshore pelagics like wahoo and tuna. Reels must contain a metal spool because the pressure of tightly packing wire eventually "blows" a plastic version. There are specialized rods equipped with a lead guide and a wire line top (swivels approximately 30 degrees on each side) which help straighten the wire during deployment. Stick with rods with large, smooth carboloy guides. Roller guides may jam and kink the wire and become susceptible to damage themselves.

RIGGING IT UP

Spooling completely with wire is expensive, therefore many anglers use a monofilament or dacron backing. Exactly what pound test backing and how much wire to spool is contingent on the species and where it's sought. A good rule of thumb is to spool on a 50-pound test backing, leaving space for about 200-feet of 40-pound test wire for most situations. Gearing for larger predators requires a switch to 80-pound test backing and about 250-feet of 50-pound test wire. There are a few ways to connect the wire and backing, the simplest via a barrel swivel that's small enough to pass through the guides yet stronger than the wire and backing (swivels are also used to replace kinks and sections of wire). A better connection comes with an Albright knot, after putting a Bimini twist in the backing and bending back part of the wire. Slide on a small egg sinker at the business end (which stops the swivel from jamming into the wire line top) before using a Haywire twist to attach the ball bearing snap swivel. Wire-line has no stretch and it's best to add about a three foot length of heavy monofilament as a shock leader. This monofilament (as heavy as 300-pound test with 50-pound test wire) usually rides between the rod's snap swivel and cigar weight

(trolling sinker). The actual leader and lure follow this trolling weight, its length varying with the species pursued. However, spooning enthusiasts use anywhere between 30 and 60 feet of leader to give their lure plenty of arc to swim within

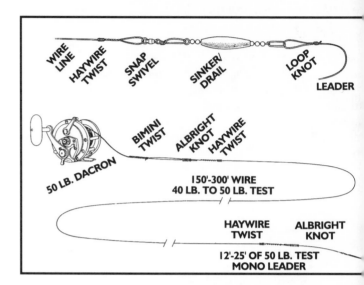

Wire line is especially popular in the Northeast, but it can produce fish anywhere when properly rigged. Be sure to cushion your reel with Dacron backing before adding the wire and monofilament leader. UPPER DRAWING: This shows how trolling drails can be added between the wire and the terminal tackle.

PUTTING IT TO WORK

Anglers can expect to penetrate about one foot of water for every ten-feet of wire at speeds no greater than five knots. That formula still applies at slightly higher speeds by choosing a heavier trolling lead. Because wire has a tendency to "unravel" on the spool, smoothly pay out a lure, perhaps backing off the drag just enough for the water pressure to carry it back (keeping tension on the spool). Anglers often mark off certain distances with dental floss, tape or a swab of Liquid Plastic to keep track of a rod's deployment.

Compared to traditional "pump and reel" techniques, wire-lining takes a bit more finesse. After a fish makes its initial run, begin retrieving line by slightly and smoothly lifting the rod and reeling on the descent. Refrain from any sharp lifts or unorthodox motions which may cause a kink, making sure to level wind the wire onto the spool.

Although trolling spoons are popular, any bait or lure will work on a wire-line. Trolling techniques can be as simple as adding an outfit to a "traditional" spread, or as specialized as power drifting a live bait alongside a wreck or ledge. Unless you're a gung-ho sub-surface troller, one wire-line outfit will do, particularly with a downrigger. Between the two devices you'll be able to cover a greater portion of the water column and fool a few extra fish.

KITE FISHING:

The fishing kite is a powerful, yet misunderstood ally of the salt water angler. Regarded as a tool that's used primarily in live-baiting sailfish, the device is by no means restricted to that species or even the use of live bait. Even its popularity is confined mainly to Southeast Florida. There re, however, some anglers who have adapted the system to popular coastal species in the Gulf of Mexico, Bermuda and the mid-Atlantic. With a little insight you can modify this deadly instrument to suit your style of fishing.

The advantage of a fishing kite is two fold. It enables an angler to present a bait to a fish in a totally different fashion. Because the kite hovers above the water, a bait can be dangled enticingly below its release clip. The vertical line angle keeps both the terminal gear and extreme dorsal region of the bait out of the water, resulting in a swimming and thrashing action that's irresistible to gamefish. The kite also permits more baits to be fished in a spread, especially in a still-drifting situation where it flies downwind of the boat.

There are four versions of fishing kites, which are square configurations comprised of a stretch of lightweight cloth

There aren't many sailfish that can turn away from a "livie" dangling beneath a fishing kite. Although the fishing kite is used mostly in this fishery, it's by no means limited to the offshore world.

over a series of hollow fiberglass supports: Light breeze (10 knots or less), Medium breeze (between 10 and 15 knots), Heavy breeze (15 and 20 knots) and Extra heavy (above 15 knots). Cloth densities and frame strengths determine the differences. There are kite rod and reel outfits on the market, but all it takes to build a quality system is a 4/0 reel and an old, stiff boat rod shortened to about four feet.

Use Dacron line because it has no stretch, filling the kite reel with either 50 or 80-pound test. Tie in a small barrel swivel 50-feet down. Slide on a Black's Kite Release Clip (available in well stocked tackle shops and marinas, or from the company in Homestead, Florida) and tie a ball bearing snap swivel onto the business end of the line. The snap swivel will attach to the kite. If you prefer fishing two baits from

a kite, tie in a larger barrel swivel 40-feet below the first swivel. Take another release clip and bore its opening with a drill bit until it slides over the smaller swivel. It will rest against the large swivel when deployed, yet retreat over the smaller one and follow the lead clip right to the ball bearing snap swivel when the kite's reeled in.

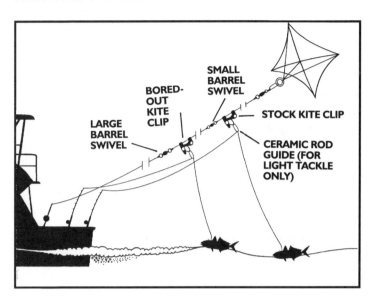

More than one bait can ride on a fishing kite. Tie in a larger barrel swivel 40-feet below the first one, then bore out the opening of the release clip so it'll slide over the smaller, lead barrel swivel. When deployed, the release clip closest to the kite will stop at its swivel, but the clip with the larger opening will have passed over it enroute to its swivel. A ceramic rod guide riding on the actual fishing line can keep light line from fouling in the kite clip. Just attach the ceramic guide to the clip and have at it.

FLYING THE BAITS

When setting the baits, fly the kite out (adjusting the small, center tab for proper balance) to the lead swivel, sliding the second release clip over it. Take the fishing line from above its double line and, after setting the right tension, insert it into the lead clip (to prevent damage to a line lighter than 20-pound test, pass it through a ceramic guide ring that'll attach to the clip). Pay out the kite to the next clip, maintaining pressure and occasionally free-spooling the loaded fishing line to keep the bait swimming in the water directly beneath its clip. Repeat the procedure with the second bait, locking down the drag on the kite reel when it's fully deployed. The closest bait should swim between 30 and 100-feet from the boat.

Constant attention keeps the live baits in an attractive position. If neglected, varying wind velocities will "lift" a kite, bringing the baits out of the water, and "lower" it, where the baits swim beneath the surface. Setting the hook depends on the species. If your quarry are "swallowers", such as sailfish, dolphin or tuna, free-spool for a few seconds before engaging the reel's drag, and then wind madly to eliminate slack. Continue winding as the line falls from the pin, setting the hook only when the fish runs against a solid drag. For "slashing" species, such as kingfish and wahoo, retrieve line immediately on the strike to set the hook(s). To re-load, simply wind the kite in until you reach the empty clip.

DON'T STOP ON TOP

An ardent live baiter takes advantage of the entire water column. In a still-drifting situation he often fishes two kite baits off the downwind side of the boat, drifts a pair of baits off the opposite gunwale (one free-lined, the other tethered to a balloon float) and sends at least one bait well into the depths on a downrigger. In a power-drift (where the motor is used to maintain headway), fly a kite among a spread of livies swimming just beneath the surface off the outriggers, complimenting it with a downrigger.

As mentioned earlier, there are applications that don't require live bait. One situation is where fish, particularly tunas, are chummed behind a boat. A flying fish, mullet, ballyhoo or even a plastic strip bait can be tethered to a kite and flown over the activity from an anchored boat (providing there's a breeze). The trick lies in skipping the dead bait across the surface as the kite is being deployed and retrieved. It's a game of labor and timing, but the results can be spectacular, especially after the fish are teased a bit.

Fishing kites are designed to perform in most wind conditions. Choose a kite rod and reel outfit that facilitates an easy and quick deployment.

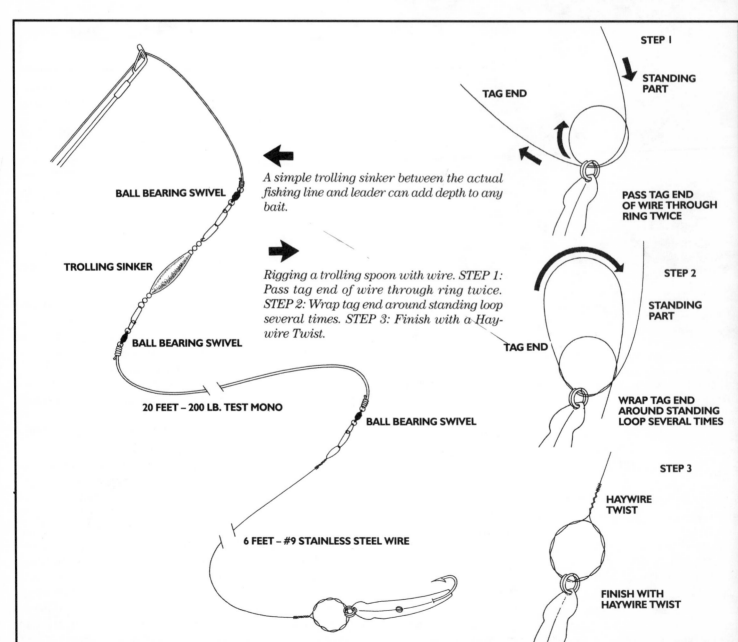

BALL BEARING SWIVEL

A simple trolling sinker between the actual fishing line and leader can add depth to any bait.

TROLLING SINKER

Rigging a trolling spoon with wire. STEP 1: Pass tag end of wire through ring twice. STEP 2: Wrap tag end around standing loop several times. STEP 3: Finish with a Haywire Twist.

BALL BEARING SWIVEL

20 FEET – 200 LB. TEST MONO

BALL BEARING SWIVEL

6 FEET – #9 STAINLESS STEEL WIRE

STEP 1

TAG END

STANDING PART

PASS TAG END OF WIRE THROUGH RING TWICE

STEP 2

STANDING PART

TAG END

WRAP TAG END AROUND STANDING LOOP SEVERAL TIMES

STEP 3

HAYWIRE TWIST

FINISH WITH HAYWIRE TWIST

APPROACH AND PRESENTATION

...now where to fish and how to master the best technique and ...u'll be that much closer to nabbing a real trophy.

...ish rely on their senses to survive in a very dangerous and ...fficult environment. Sight, sound, and smell mesh togeth- ... to help each critter find food, avoid becoming a meal for ...me huskier predator, and stick around long enough to ...pawn. By nature, marine creatures remain suspicious and ...ary. One wrong move and they swim no more. Countering ...is, a fish must be an opportunist to find sufficient food, fo- ...using on a multitude of sources.

Anglers concentrate their efforts on choosing the right ...ckle and employing effective techniques. In the process, ...ey often overlook critical tactics that rank as essential in- ...redients for success. Approach and presentation head the ...st. If you can put a bait or lure in front of a fish in a natural ...anner without that animal realizing you're in the neigh- ...orhood, your score will soar. That concept outweighs the ...pecifics of the offering you choose. Any critter alerted to ...ur presence becomes much more difficult to fool. It may ...ot bolt away in panic or even give any indication of alarm, ...ut it is still incredibly tough to catch that fish. Unfortunately, ...ost of us fish waters too opaque to reveal what lies below ...e surface, so we tend to ignore the basics of approach.

MAKING A GOOD APPROACH

Consistently successful anglers share a common trait. They are totally and continuously aware of everything happening around them on the water. Above the surface, these veterans rely on sight and sound. Below, they monitor depth sounders to follow bottom contours and depth curves.

The practical aspects of approach begin before one gets to the chosen area. If you're going to work a shoreline, you don't want to arrive on a course that will send a mountainous wake from your boat crashing into the sector you plan to cast or troll. Disturb a fish and its senses go into red alert.

A better route would direct the wake away from prime habitat. Obviously, it pays to cut the throttle some distance from the target and idle up slowly or use some other means of propulsion such as an electric motor or a pushpole.

Shallow water enthusiasts enjoy the advantage of visually monitoring the results of approach. Not only have they learned to shut down a considerable distance from where they plan to fish, but they'll also drift or pole on a course tailored to intercept anything they see.

Try not to run an engine over the area you will be fishing, particularly in the shallows. If you are drifting and casting, work your way as silently as possible into deeper water. Then, run a considerable distance offshore and circle back to the starting point so you can make another drift. That way, you won't alert any denizen in the path of your drift.

Use a quiet approach when fishing shallow waters. Never run hard and back off at your destination. Instead, ease into the area.

BREAKING SCHOOLS

Picking fish from a breaking school seldom poses a problem until the second boat appears on the scene. The chemistry instantly changes from simple excitement to complex competition. Skippers press harder, shouldering and shoving their boats until they crowd and annoy their quarry. New boats race to the area with throttles pinned to the stops, emulating the charge of a cavalry troop with sabres swinging in the air.

The depths provide the only sanctuary for the fish once boats run through the ranks and they quickly disappear. A more logical approach suggests that throttles be pulled back a respectable distance from the melee. You can close the re-

The same rule holds true with nearshore fish: Keep the boat at bay and "bait" only the fringes. You'll keep the "action" alive much long…

maining gap at idle speed. The key lies in lingering on the fringes, casting toward the commotion. If you're trolling, work the edges. You don't have to drag the baits through the center of the commotion to buy a strike.

Should you happen upon this scenario with only a minimum of other boats piloted by captains who exhibit common sense, try to ease around the school, take up a position in their path, shut the engines off, and let the fish come to you.

BAITING A FISH ON THE SURFACE

Big game anglers often encounter sailfish, marlin, sharks, tuna, and other species tailing downsea or simply swimming along the surface. The basic approach dictates that you present the baits to the fish rather than the boat. To do this, run parallel to your quarry with the trolled baits positioned astern. You may want to lengthen the distance on the long bait on the side that will bear on the fish.

Nudge the throttles just a tad so the boat speed is slig… ly faster than the swim rate of the fish. Once the boat h… passed beyond the fish, easy the helm toward the fish's tra… That will swing the long bait right in front of the target. If y… run over the fish first, it's going to be much more difficult… entice, assuming, of course, you don't put it down perm… nently.

TROLLING PATTERNS

Whether you concentrate on the inshore or offsho… grounds, establish a meaningful trolling pattern based … current, wave pattern, and underwater terrain. Work a se…

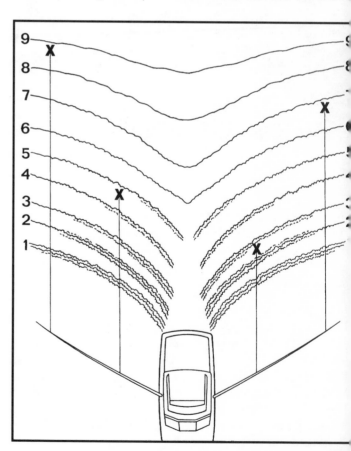

Keeping a school of offshore fish on the surface requires discipline and a systematic approach. Determine which way they're headed and, if you're trolling, try to let the baits intercept the lead fringes.

Many top offshore captains swear that fine-tuning a lure spre… is much more important than picking colors. They'll fish t… lures on the front side of the waves created by their wake. E… perience tells them which wave patterns work best behind the… boat.

or and then move on to the next. You will probably want to roll with the seas, across them, and against the waves. The same holds with current.

If you find a dropoff, try paralleling it, working from shallow to deep, and then drag from deep to shallow. Should you raise a fish, be sure you mentally note the direction you were moving in relation to these factors.

Certain species hold around bottom structure. Usually, you'll find them on the downcurrent side, but dead spots in the water flow occur on the upcurrent side. Try both directions, using your depth sounder to spot any concentration of fish.

Remember that a wreck or an artificial reef falls into the category of bottom structure. Fish may hold close to the configuration or, during periods of slower current flow, venture some distance from it.

REEFS AND DROPOFFS

Bottom bouncers and deep jiggers probe a reefline or dropoff with a game plan. If you can achieve a drift parallel to the dropoff, your offerings will be in the most productive zone on a continuous basis. The next choice centers on a drift from shallow to deep. That way, if you do hook a fish, the angle of the line will help to pull it away from any obstruction. A drift toward a reef means that the fish has an easier task of reaching bottom, because the boat is moving shallower all the time.

ON FOOT

Shorebound anglers face their own set of challenges. If you wade, the rings of water radiating outward as you take each step sound the alarm for fish. They quickly sense the displacement of water and know that something threatening is taking place. When you do wade, move as slowly as possible, minimizing rings and ripples.

Even on land, your steps send sound waves and vibrations into the water as you approach the edge of an estuary. Fish sense these and move away from shore toward deeper water. It's important to approach any body of water carefully, walking as if eggshells lay beneath your feet. And, don't walk right up to the edge before you cast. Hang back a few feet as you make your first presentations.

Fish are acutely aware of movement and they see very well. When you stand on the edge of a seawall or on the bank and start to cast, the rod looms even higher than your body. If the water has any clarity, your quarry may be able to spot that movement and react to it.

Try an experiment the next time you see a school of baitfish or even a predator close to shore. Stand quietly and observe. Then, make a sudden movement such as raising your arm and watch what happens. You will become convinced immediately that the school detected your presence.

PRESENTATION

Successful presentation involves nothing more than putting a bait or lure in front of a fish in a natural and realistic manner. In a predator/prey relationship, the predator expects its prey to move away once it detects the attack. If the bait fails to move, the attack will be broken off.

Shorebound anglers must also plan their approach. It may take plenty of finesse to buy a strike if the fish aren't feeding madly.

The intended victim does not charge the predator in nature. That's an unnatural act that will panic the larger fish. If a bait or lure moves toward the fish you intend to catch, it will flee the scene. Memorize this principle; it's that critical.

On the clear, tropical flats, this lesson takes on visual meaning. Textbooks instruct anglers to cast in front of and beyond a cruising fish. Picture a bonefish swimming from left to right. Your cast lands about 6 feet in front of the fish and 3 feet beyond its intended path. You start the retrieve and the fish flushes.

From your perspective, the lure would pass well in front of the fish and clear its nose by a couple of feet. That's not the way the bonefish reads the scene. Here comes something on an intercept course. If it were prey, it would take off in the other direction. Since it's still coming, the fish is going to take evasive action.

The correct technique is simple. Reel quickly until the lure is right in the path of the bonefish. Then, start the retrieve as if the lure were trying to escape. That should do it.

SIGHT FISHING

Successful sight fishing demands two judgement calls. Making the first cast count ranks as an essential element of presentation. Most anglers reach out to their extreme casting range when they can see the target. Accuracy suffers. If you wait until the fish is too close, you won't have a chance for a second shot. Not all experts agree, but some of the best believe you should wait until you can put that first presentation right on the money. You don't have to worry about a second cast if the first one does the job.

To catch fish, you have to take chances. The second decision centers on how close to the fish you present the bait. If you're cautious, you reduce the risk of spooking your quarry, but you also increase the odds that the fish won't see the offering. It's a tradeoff, but knowledgable guides prefer an aggressive approach. Get the bait to the fish and make that critter eat. Frequently, strikes result from reflexive action, particularly when the predator suddenly sees prey trying to escape.

TIDE AND CURRENT

Tides and currents occur every day in the lives of fish and they instinctively use them to their advantage. Fish hold

Fish have a keen sense of smell, but a running current is essential when chumming; It takes the scent and tidbits to them.

in one spot by facing into the current. Many species feed into the current for three reasons: swimming stability when searching for a meal, the flow of water carries food to them, and it also spreads the scents and smell tracks that help them locate goodies.

To make a presentation look natural, the offering should approach the fish with the current as if it were being swept along by the force of the water. You might make it appear as if the bait were struggling against the flow, but obviously, a tiny critter wouldn't make much progress.

Even on the flats where you can see cruising bonefish, tarpon, redfish, or other denizens, make the cast upcurrent so that the fly or lure swings down toward the target. If you're working a shoreline, understand that predators take up stations at ambush points where the flow brings the meal to them. A retrieve from the wrong direction would appear to be attacking the predator and the results would be disappointing.

Speed of retrieve can be critical when dealing with a current. One erroneously senses that the lure is moving faster in relation to the fish than it really is. It's being pushed by the current, but so is a moving fish. Sometimes, you have to increase the retrieve rate to make it seem as if the lure was trying to get away from the big fellow.

If you happen to be casting a shoreline, the stage of the tide may make a difference. On rising water, fish tend to push back against the shoreline. That may become a problem when there are mangroves or overhanging trees. More water means that the fish are harder to reach because they move back where you can't get a clear cast. With a flooding tide, each presentation should be as close to the edges of tree branches or shorelines as possible. A foot or two may make a difference between catching fish and merely enjoying a casting session.

On the same subject, when casting to structure, the key lies in dropping the bait or lure beyond the spot where you expect the fish to be holding. All of us have the tendency to aim right for the structure. The sound of a lure plopping over the head of a fish may spook it or at least warn of danger. You want the retrieve to take the offering right past the fish, but the bait must drop in a neutral zone.

CHUMMING

To chum effectively, a current must be running. If you are trying to draw fish from structure such as a wreck, anchor upcurrent of the fish and let the flowing water take the scent and tidbits back to your quarry. The slick must be continuous and that means without interruption, even when all hands are busy fighting fish.

One can always find exceptions, but the best presentation in a chum slick is a dead drift. With natural bait, it's an art to match the drift rate of the chum. You achieve this by constantly feeding controlled slack line. When the current eases before a tide change, try going to tiny hooks and much smaller pieces of bait. The chum is falling toward the bottom faster than a large, baited hook.

In some waters, chum attracts swarms of smaller fish that feed frantically on the free meal. Oversized predators hear this commotion and swim over to investigate. Anglers stand ready with rod in hand watching the water for signs of the husky critters. That's when the cast is made and, in this instance, the lure is usually retrieved. If you are using live bait, put it in front of the predator and get ready.

A WORD ABOUT BAITS AND RETRIEVES

Natural bait should always be the freshest you can obtain. Fresh bait consistently outfishes frozen bait that has been thawed. Researchers suggest that you use the smallest bait that will attract the fish you seek. Their reasoning is that it's easier for a fish to wolf down a smaller morsel. Consider, however, that sometimes it takes a larger bait to get a fish's attention.

Experiments indicate that when a school of fish feeds frantically on a source of bait and suddenly seems satiated, one should switch to a larger bait. The introduction of a more satisfying meal often turns on the fish one more time.

When you're bouncing a bucktail along the bottom or working an artificial lure, keep in mind that 2 or 3-inch critters don't make 4-foot hops. The same thinking applies to plugs. Small fish don't go very far with only a few tailbeats. The movement may be quick, but it has to be in rapid, short spurts.

BREAKING FISH

Feasting fish on the surface might look like a barroom brawl, but you'll discover that organization and direction exist. When a breaking school maintains a direction, few individuals will turn back to grab a bait or lure. They'll charge anything in front of them, but seldom change direction.

Once the boat is positioned ahead of the pack and well on the fringes, make your casts toward the school. Predators must isolate their prey and will attack a single victim. As the bait or lure clears the melee, it stands out and will be hit instantly. Live bait should be fished around the fringes of the school, but it will also bring action right in the middle of free-swimming bait. The reason is that the hooked offering gives off distress vibrations and swims differently. It's easy for a predator to isolate it and attack.

If you're trolling, try to pick a course so that the baits travel in the same direction as the school. You're more prone to get strikes. By going against the flow, you limit your chances. Keep in mind that plenty of fish remain below the

f you're working fish that are corralling bait in shallow waters, try sending an offering to the bottom. Many times the bigger and ~~marter~~ smarter fish are lurking behind, feeding on the maimed and dead baits.

~~urface~~ surface on the edges of the school. You don't have to disturb ~~he~~ the main body to consistently pick fish from the sides.

TENDING BOTTOM

Bottom dwellers spend most of their lives within a few ~~eet~~ feet of the sea floor. Reaching them seems easy, but it often ~~lemands~~ demands considerable skill. From a drifting boat or when ~~lealing~~ dealing with a strong current, the flow sweeps lure or bait up-~~vard~~ward, often carrying it well above the fish. Learning to tend ~~ottom~~ bottom becomes a practiced skill. One must develop a touch ~~r~~ or a feel that transmits the message the lead is on the bottom.

In many situations, the sinker or jig should be just heavy ~~enough~~ enough to reach the bottom. You want it to bounce and move ~~o~~ so that it covers a wider area, rather than have it hold in one ~~pot~~ spot as an anchor. With a sinker, the technique is to lift the ~~od~~ rod tip slightly and then monitor the drop. You should be ~~ible~~ able to actually feel bottom. In deeper water, you'll see the ~~ine~~ line go slack for an instant. If this doesn't happen, you have ~~o~~ to let out more line until it does. It requires constant atten-~~ion~~tion to keep the bait in the productive zone.

Jigging takes several forms. In the most common, one ~~lrops~~ drops the leadhead directly over the side of the boat and al-~~ows~~lows it to free-fall until it reaches bottom. You then have the ~~ption~~ option of retrieving it all the way to the surface or keeping it

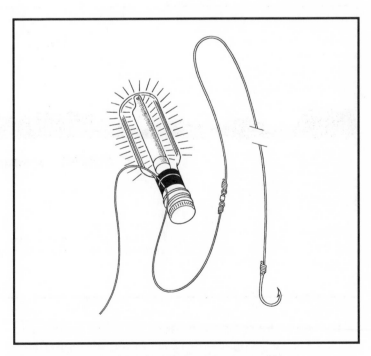

Have you ever tried an illuminated float at night? The light can attract bait and toll in a gamefish. A small bottle or balloon, a Cyalume light and a strip of tape are all that's required.

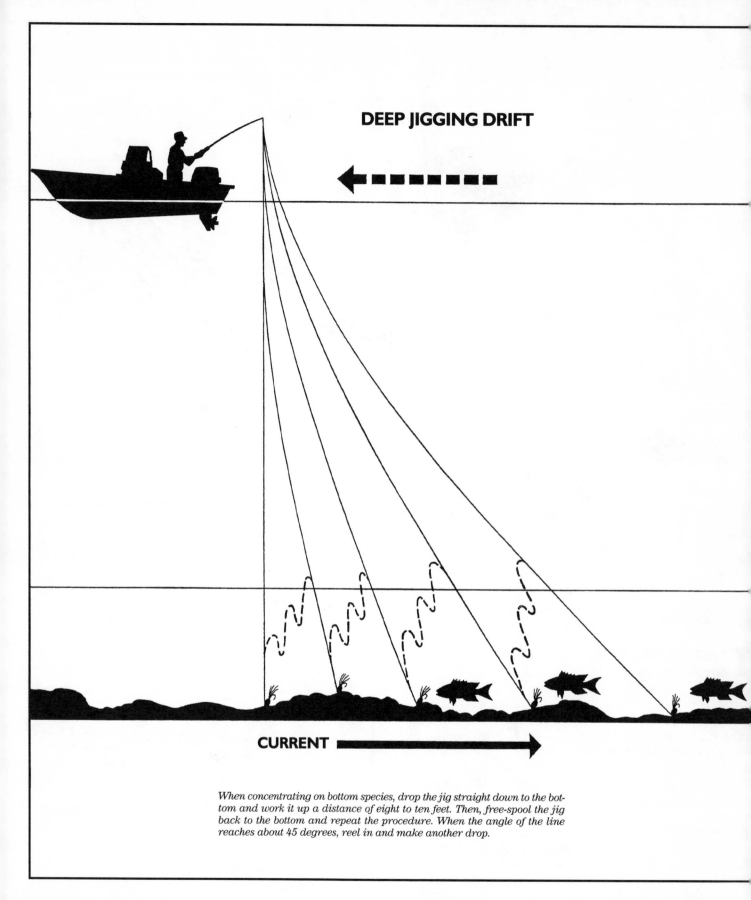

DEEP JIGGING DRIFT

CURRENT

When concentrating on bottom species, drop the jig straight down to the bottom and work it up a distance of eight to ten feet. Then, free-spool the jig back to the bottom and repeat the procedure. When the angle of the line reaches about 45 degrees, reel in and make another drop.

on the bottom for as long as possible. If you choose the latter, you will have to let out more line after every few upward rod movements. When the angle of the line entering the water decreases from 90 degrees to perhaps 45 degrees, it's time to reel in and make another drop.

Presentation ranks as one of the key ingredients fo catching fish. If you ignore even the smallest detail, you d minish your chances accordingly. Focus on presentation an many of the other complexities of a meaningful day on th water will take care of themselves.

11 GETTING STARTED IN SALT WATER FLY FISHING

[f]or some, there is no better thrill than pursuing bonefish with a [f]lyrod.

Saltwater fly fishing quickly leads to an insatiable quest, adding a new and challenging dimension to time spent on the water. The key lies in keeping it in perspective. The tackle imposes certain limitations. Trying to force casts into the throat of a gale feeds frustration for salt-encrusted aficionados as well as beginners. Searching the seas with a fly rod hour after hour taxes the strongest arm. A more sensible approach leads to opportunity fishing. Find the fish first and then switch to fly tackle.

Any species known to charge and engulf an artificial lure becomes fair game for the marine feather merchant. An array of fly lines with an assortment of sink rates allows anglers to probe the depths as well as the surface. The introduction of a 20-pound (10 kg) tippet class by the IGFA opens new vistas for those determined to wrestle critters the size of pilot whales on regulation fly gear.

CHOOSING THE ROD

In today's fly fishing world, graphite reigns as the material of choice for virtually all assignments. Fiberlass (S-glass) certainly has a place, particularly for those who must establish budgetary restraints on equipment purchases. Cane rods no longer find their way to ocean or estuary, except in isolated instances by diehard traditionalists.

Buy the best flyrod you can afford. The right choice is worth the investment in terms of casting performance and fish-fighting ability. All graphite is not the same. At least three generations of graphite fly rods have been unveiled with the fourth just around the corner. Each represents a significant improvement in performance, based on material. To be effective, a fly rod must combine material with engineering. Graphite cannot bridge the gap when the design falls short.

Choosing a rod really starts with an analysis of the flies you intend to use. Since the weight of the fly line carries the fly, you have to settle on a fly line heavy enough to handle the flies you plan to fish. Each fly rod is engineered to handle a

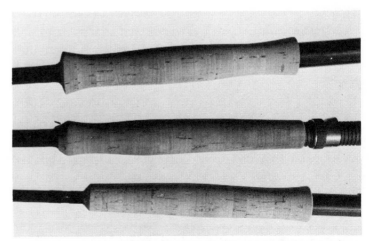

The Full Wells grip (top) and the Half Wells (middle) rank as two of the most popular grips on flyrods. Some manufacturers insist on inverting the Half Wells (bottom) or using a cigar shape grip. This is more difficult to hold.

fly line of a specific weight. You have a little leeway in some cases by going one size heavier or lighter than recommended. For most applications, the line weight specified on the rod is the one to follow.

Recovery ranks as the primary factor in selecting a casting tool. Wherever the tip of the rod travels, the fly line follows, creating shock waves in the line. The best rods boast a dampening effect that reduces tip vibrations to a minimum. To check recovery, hold the rod in front of you parallel to the floor with the butt at your belt buckle. Snap the rod sharply while watching the tip. The tip should absorb the shock quickly with only minor side-to-side travel.

Graphite fostered the development of longer and lighter fly rods. A 9-foot rod has become the standard for marine work. Some of the new 20-pound class rods are 8-feet or 8-1/2-feet to increase the fighting effectiveness. For casting, it's more difficult to turn over a 9-1/2 or 10-foot rod in a wind and the longer length can prove more fatiguing when blind casting.

Three different fly reel sizes will cover the marine waterfront for the feather merchant. Most anglers refer to these sizes as bonefish, tarpon, and marlin. One should choose a direct drive reel in the small size. It's a matter of choice with the larger models.

Most saltwater fly rods are equipped with an extension butt to keep the reel away from one's body. A 2-inch butt makes sense, but anything longer usually gets in the way and positions the reel too far from the body.

Rod guides also become a critical consideration. Snake guides outperform all other types. You want the largest snakes made on a marine fly rod. Manufacturers usually rely on a ceramic guide for the first or stripping guide and that's fine. Beyond that, don't settle for anything but snake guides.

With only two fly rods, a 9-weight for most situations and a 12-weight or 13-weight as a fighting tool, one can fish comfortably in oceans and estuaries around the world. That isn't to say you can't use an 8-weight, 10-weight, or 11-weight, but rather to point out the place to start. The trend today leans toward three-piece or four-piece travelling models that can be carried aboard an airliner. They are available in a full range of sizes up through 13-weight.

FLY REELS

Single action fly reels (one revolution of the handle pr duces one revolution of the spool) set the standard for mari fly fishing. Multiplying models with gear ratios in excess of have been around for many years and you'll probably s more entries in the seasons ahead. Tradition dictates sing action.

The two primary requirements focus on adequate li capacity for a fly line plus the necessary backing and a smoo drag. Fly reels boast so much internal space that smoo drags have become commonplace. Almost all of the reels the market perform well and the decision often necks dow to a question of price and "how good is good?"

Fly reels are machined in several sizes, but three me attention. The smallest holds about 200 yards of braide Dacron backing plus an 8-weight or 9-weight fly line. It is o ten referred to as a bonefish model. The tarpon model mid-size reel handles at least 250 yards of 30-pound te Dacron backing plus a 12-weight or 13-weight fly line. B game fly reels spool at least 400 yards of 30-pound backin plus the fly line. They were designed for those anglers see ing to take a billfish, tuna, large shark or other oversize denizen on fly.

It doesn't make sense to some anglers to cast a fly r with the right hand (or left) and then switch hands to re when battling a fish. Unless you are truly ambidextrou cranking with the weaker hand is a mistake. You can tu the handle faster and longer with your stronger hand. If yc are right-handed, opt for a right-hand retrieve on the ree

One more option requires a decision. Most reels are o fered in direct drive models (the handle turns backwar when line is pulled off the spool) or anti-reverse models (th handle remains stationary). On the bonefish size reel, the rect drive makes sense. If you set the drag to compensa for a light leader tippet, you may not be able to retrieve lir with a direct drive reel after a fish makes a long run. For th mid-size and large reels, you can go either way. The advantag of direct drive lies in the knowledge that you are recoverir line whenever you turn the handle. The disadvantage is tha the handle may rap your knuckles if you don't get your har out of the way fast enough.

FLY LINE

A uniform labelling system makes it easy to select th right line for any assignment. It deals with taper, weight, an density in that order. For saltwater work, a weight forward f line works best (designated WF). That indicates that most the weight and the taper are concentrated in the first 30 fee A shooting taper (ST) is only 30-feet long, but the design pa allels that of a weight forward. With a shooting taper, yc add your own running line; in a weight forward, the runnir line is an integral part.

Weight is determined by actually weighing the first 3 feet in grains and then assigning a number from 1 to 15 (c more). The higher the number, the heavier the line. Tha means that a WF-10 (weight forward 10-weight) weighs mor than a WF-8.

Density completes the picture. If the line floats, that is ir dicated by the letter F. A fly line labelled WF-9-F is a weigh forward, 9-weight, floater. Sinking lines carry the letter S while very slow sinking lines are termed I for intermediate. Since sinking lines now come in several densities, you'll come across designators that indicate the rate.

Combination lines (F/S) allow the front portion to sink, while the rear section floats. The first line you should buy is a weight forward floater with a weight designation that matches the recommendation on your rod. You can add additional lines later.

BACKING AND LEADERS

Backing not only serves as an extension of the fly line when a fish makes a long run, but helps to build a core on the reel that increases spool diameter. Braided Dacron remains the backing of choice because it lays flat on the spool and has very low stretch (less than 10%). Tailor the breaking strength of the backing to the leader tippet. If the tippet is 12-pound test or less, you can use 20 pound Dacron backing. Heavier tippets require 30 pound backing. As a rule of thumb, use 20 pound backing on a 9-weight outfit and 30 pound on a 12-weight.

To attach backing to flyline, splice a loop in the Dacron or tie a Bimini twist, leaving a loop at least six inches long. Strip the coating off the tag end of the fly line using a piece of 10-pound test mono and bend the core of the flyline back to form a loop. Serve the tag end of the loop against the fly line using a fly tying bobbin and thread. Whip-finish the end and coat the connection with Pliobond or another rubber-based cement.

The basic saltwater leader starts with a butt section of 30-pound or 40-pound mono. This can be attached to the fly line with a nail knot and coated with Pliobond or you can serve a loop in the front end of the fly line just as you did to the tag end. If you choose the latter method, put a surgeon's loop in the end of the butt section and interlock the two loops. That way, you can change butt sections quickly.

The class tippet is the lightest section of the leader in terms of breaking strength. It should be at least 15 inches long. A shock tippet may be heavier mono or even wire depending on the species. This is usually 12 inches long. For a more delicate presentation, leaders are tapered by knotting sections of monofilament in decreasing diameters (and break strength).

The shorter the leader, the easier it is to cast. Any leader over 9 feet becomes much more difficult to handle. The purpose of the leader lies in keeping the fly line away from the fish. Longer leaders may be necessary for some shallow water species, particularly on slick calm days. If you use a sinking line, the leader should be relatively short. Otherwise, the line sinks, but the leader tends to float, taking the fly above the fish.

PICKING THE RIGHT FLY

The imagination of fly tyers seems to be the only limiting factor in the development of saltwater patterns. Presentation frequently outweighs the choice of the actual fly. If you put it in front of a fish in a realistic manner, chances are the fish will strike.

Size and silhouette of the pattern rank high in importance. Pick a pattern that appoximates the length and shape of the preferred baitfish. Keep in mind that smaller and less

Any streamer fly can be made into a popper instantly by slipping a cork on the leader and sliding it over the eye of the hook.

bulky flies cast more easily. Fully dressed flies work well in off-color water. If you want a fly to sink quickly, it has to be weighted, but the sparser the tie, the faster it will sink. Weighted flies can be essential in water as shallow as 18 inches, particularly when you want it to reach bottom in front of a cruising bonefish.

Hook size is critical. You will experience difficulty setting any hook larger than 4/0. Opt for a relatively light wire hook and be sure to sharpen it to increase its penetration effectiveness.

Most saltwater flies are tied on stainless steel hooks to retard rusting. Contrary to popular belief, no hook rusts out quickly underwater, regardless of the metal used.

Color becomes another consideration. Too many anglers concern themselves with subtle shading. Think in terms of light and dark. If you use a relatively light-colored pattern and it isn't working or you can see fish refusing it, switch to a dark pattern (or vice versa). It's fascinating to observe competing tournament fishermen. Each insists on a carefully selected pattern and color. The problem lies in the fact that no two anglers fish the same pattern or the same color and most of them catch fish.

LET'S GO FISHING

Fly fishing takes two forms: sight casting to fish you can see and blind casting designed to cover as much water as possible. In the first instance, speed and accuracy become paramount. You only have a few seconds to get the fly to the fish and it has to be on target. Too close and you spook your quarry to the next county; play it safe and the fish may never see the fly. Think of it as walking a tightrope between aggressiveness and caution.

The wonderful part about sight fishing is that you get instant feedback on the results. You can tell if the presentation was good, but that critter turned its nose up at the fly. Repeat that scenario two or three times and you had better switch to another pattern.

Dealing with moving targets and hampering wind takes practice. That's why there is a difference between fly casting

A fly-caught bonefish is about to gain its freedom. The fly must sink to the bottom quickly where a bonefish will spot it easily. Anglers carry a selection of weighted and non-weighted patterns so that they can match water depth and conditions.

on the lawn and fly fishing on the water. Your goal lies in putting the fly in front of the fish and not the fly line. A fly line falling across the back of a fish will send it scurrying for safety. With a single fish, keeping the line away may not be difficult. The challenge increases when you must deal with a school, particularly when you fail to see school members that happen to be swimming between you and your target.

Even if you manage to get the fly to the fish, retrieve can be a problem. How fast you strip the fly can make a difference. Frequently, the angler thinks he is taking the fly away from the fish, but the offering is barely moving. With some species, it may only require minor movement, but each fish reacts differently. If a fish follows a slow moving fly but won't eat it, speed it up.

Blind casting may be a common term, but rates as a poor choice of words. You cannot see your quarry, but that doesn't mean you simply toss the fly at random. It's a systematic exercise of long, probing casts executed to cover the maximum amount of water in the most effective manner. You may start with short casts and lengthen them. Perhaps you first efforts are angled off the bow of the boat with later casts working back toward the stern. On a drift, you want to constantly cover new water.

If you're determined to succeed at saltwater fly fishing start by rigging a fly rod or two before you leave the dock. Make this an essential part of any preparation. Once you locate a concentration of fish and have taken a few via another method, switch to the fly rod. You know you're working over fish and that should give you both incentive and confidence. If you begin to tire or find yourself getting sloppy, simply stop. Go back to the other type of tackle until you're ready to try it again.

THE MOMENT OF TRUTH

Once the cast is made, the butt of the rod should be at your belt buckle with the tip pointing directly at the fly. You retrieve by stripping line, not by moving the rod. With the tip pointing at the fly, you're always ready to make another cast in a hurry or set the hook on a strike.

If you feel a strike or see the fish eat the fly, your first reaction is a sharp tug with your stripping hand just as if you were double-hauling during a cast. The tug is often enough to bury the barb in a soft-mouthed fish, but it does more than that. You learn instantly whether there is a fish on the other end. If there isn't, you have only moved the fly a few feet and can continue the retrieve. By lifting the rod at the first indication, you pull the fly away from a fish and often snatch it out of the water.

Assuming you feel resistance when you tug on the line, merely sweep the rod across your body parallel to the water and the hook should be set. On fish that have mouths lined with cinder block, strike several times on the sweep.

A fish of any size will start to pull line through your stripping hand. This is a critical moment. Forget the fish. Your first and only concern is the loose fly line at your feet. Make a ring with the thumb and forefinger of your stripping hand and lead the line into the first guide. By looking down, you will avoid tangles or getting the line caught around an object, thus preventing a breakoff. Once the fish is on the reel, you can fight it just as you would with spinning or conventional tackle.

ONE LAST WORD

Fly fishing represents more than just another angling method. It marks a commitment to a philosophy in which the catch actually becomes incidental to the total experience. Being on the water with a fly rod in hand manufactures its own rewards. When one selects the fly rod as his tackle of choice, he really announces without uttering a word that he has reached an enviable plateau in the hierarchy of angling. No other combination of equipment signals the same accomplishment.

Take your fly rod and challenge every species you can find. That's the only way to really learn the intricacies of fly fishing. In the process, you'll enjoy a higher level of enjoyment than you dreamed possible.

This is what it's all about: the opportunity to battle and beat a trophy fish. This blue marlin has been tagged and is about to be released.

There's a special feeling that belongs solely to the offshore angler. As he diligently adjusts churning baits or lures into an attractive pattern and sets his sights on finding fish, the anticipation of connecting with an oversized gladiator keeps him in full alert and ready for the challenge. He knows it could happen at anytime, no matter how slow the fishing may be.

A billfish or tuna exploding on a bait and the distinctive sound of line crackling off the reel have a way of making time stand still. The angler races for the rod while his team gets ready to clear the cockpit for the chase. With the angler strapped into the chair, the boat is slipped out of gear and then into reverse to regain line. The angler reels frantically to close the gap until the fish surges ahead, the maddening pace or control continuing until the fish finally sounds and settles into a slow, grueling give and take battle. Both opponents grow weary, but the angler's state of mind and adrenalin flowing through his body give him the ability to forget about the pain, an edge that'll eventually overcome the fish. The sight of the behemoth thrashing on the leader alongside the boat is worth another load of adrenalin. You admire it, warm with satisfaction, and decide whether to boat it or set it free, hopefully to reproduce and, perhaps, thrill another angler.

There's a certain amount of luck in offshore fishing. How many times have you heard the stories about novices who towed lures or baits on inferior tackle and caught a fish that would make even the most seasoned professional cringe with jealousy? There's no telling where that trophy fish may be in the wide open ocean, putting everyone on a somewhat equal level. However, if the score cards were tallied up at the end of a season, the experienced anglers will undoubtedly shine. There's no formula to luck, but consistency takes a thorough knowledge of the targeted species (including it's migratory habits), an acute ability to read the water and a knack at selecting and fishing the right baits.

COMMUNICATION:

Communication is essential in learning the whereabouts of fish. Successful captains and anglers often communicate with others along their coast, sharing valuable information that can reduce the time spent in finding fish. Take sailfish, for example: If the main body of fish is reported off of Stuart, Florida, a Palm Beach based angler some 40-miles south will monitor the weather and form his fishing plans accordingly. If the wind hails from a northerly quadrant, he'll expect the fish to be farther south the following day. He'll run about 20-miles north and try to intercept them as they push south. As long as the wind holds from the north, the fish should continue pushing south with favorable water temperatures, possibly invading Palm Beach waters within two days. However, if the wind remains predominantly from the southeast, with no signs of an approaching cold front, he understands that he must travel at least 40-miles north to better his odds.

By learning information like the depth the fish have been traveling in, their average size and the most effective baits and techniques, the inquisitive angler can also narrow his

As small as it seems, the VHF radio plays a big role in offshore fishing. Communication with other anglers can help reduce the time spent in locating fish.

"window" of effort. Instead of trying to locate fish over a broad depth range between 80 and 400-feet of water, he's likely to do well by concentrating on depths between 200 and 260-feet – if the fish are reported in 240-feet of water. However, there are always exceptions. If bait seems particularly thick in certain zones, take time to fish there.

Keeping track of fish migrations before you set forth will give you a head start on the competition. All it takes is to establish contact with a few individuals at your extremes. Don't be shy about using the VHF on the grounds, monitoring the activity. Providing you're honest and return accurate information you can bank on these contacts for years to come. It only stands to reason that the longer and harder you fish a fertile area, the better your success ratio will be.

THE GAMEPLAN:

Not unlike a professional football coach, some of the most successful anglers never set forth without a gameplan. They'll formulate an idea on where they'll begin fishing (based on communication and their latest voyages), the size of baits and lures they'll use and the most effective techniques. They leave little to chance. If the primary plan isn't producing, they know how to read the water and alter their strategies accordingly.

A great day on the water begins the evening before. It may seem like a tiresome chore, but a variety of tackle should be rigged to cover a number of opportunities. All outfits should carry fresh knot systems, and spinning and bait-casting outfits should be rigged with jigs, plain bait hooks and surface plugs on both monofilament and wire leaders. If a fish is spotted at the surface, or a school happens around the boat, the angler can readily grab a rod and seize the opportunity.

Bait and lure size should be determined by the weight of the fish passing through and the angler's tackle. For example, if dolphin are averaging less than 10-pounds, small to medium size baits will account for much more action and better hook-up percentages than large baits. A big dolphin readily consumes a small bait, but it's often difficult for an average size fish to contain a big offering. Furthermore, the scaled down hooks in small baits are a lot easier to set on 20 and 30-pound class gear.

If you're only interested in chasing trophies, eliminating the small baits draws fewer strikes from average-size fish. Sticking with the dolphin example, big cows and bulls readily attack horse (extra large) ballyhoo. However, school fish often shy away from them, leaving the angler free to pursue his goal. A good compromiser mixes the baits, sizing most to catch average size fish. Yet you can count on seeing one that's exceptionally large and another that's very small, since the odd size baits are sometimes singled out by gamefish.

Whatever baits or lures you decide upon, rig them in advance. Don't fall into the trap by rationalizing that there's plenty of time enroute to the fishing grounds to prepare baits and tackle, no matter how far the run may be. There's no

There are two types of structure: hard (reefs, ledges, hump etc.) and suspended (weedlines, FADs, boards, etc.). This hu bull dolphin came from under a weedline loaded with bait

This is not the time to worry about a weak spot in the line or leader system! Go over the tackle, rig the baits and form a gameplan the evening before.

such luxury. A sharp captain spends that time monitoring the water for signs that can lead to fish.

HOW TO READ THE WATER

For the uninitiated, offshore trolling can be a boring proposition: they reach their destination, toss the baits over,

and plug along hoping to find fish. If the action isn't hot, the continue trucking blindly across the ocean, rationalizing th the fish just aren't around. If they only knew what they' missing!

Take a hard look at a dedicated offshore fishing m chine. Whether it's a 55-foot, million dollar sportfisherman a 24-foot trailerable center console, it's apt to have a surfa water temperature gauge, loran or GPS capability, digit depth sounder and a quality fishfinder. The array of ele tronics should be a dead-giveaway that the entire water c umn must be scrutinized to find fish. If an angler consul these electronics and factors in visual signs and fishing r ports, he'll be that much closer to uncovering action. By b ing aware of the surroundings, both above and below th surface, the vast ocean doesn't seem so intimidating.

When an angler nears a destination, he should che the fishfinder and pay attention to what's going on arour him.

The visual signs in question are diving birds, rips, scho ing fish and bait, activity which is usually very obvious. Hov ever, uncovering signs that aren't plainly visible is a chara teristic of a good angler. He watches the fishfinder f concentrations of bait and the surface water temperatu gauge for any fluctuations, taking time to fish these areas they're promising.

Water temperature is crucial in determining whe gamefish may be. Monitored religiously in the northeas pockets of rapid temperature change caused by the Gu

tream, warm eddies and weather patterns are productive
r tuna, shark and billfish. The edges of these gradients,
here warm offshore waters meet a much cooler inshore
helf water, can be incredible fishing spots. While tempera-
ure changes aren't as dramatic in southern waters, a full de-
ree or two difference can signify the edge of the Gulf Stream
a loop current. These "edges" are unstable wedges with-
the environment where different currents and water tem-
eratures oppose each other. They tend to gather bait and
igger feeding blitzes. As dramatic as these temperature
reaks sound, they're sometimes not distinguishable by the
uman eye (i.e. color changes, rips). An effective method of
nding these areas is through forecasters offering satellite
terpretations. They can provide accurate sea surface tem-
erature charts that are updated daily, some versions even
sting loran coordinates.

Structure, such as peaks and contours along the ocean
oor, is held in high esteem because bait and gamefish con-
regate there. Each region has its own criteria that make
eir prominent points "turn on" (i.e. currents washing
gainst them, outgoing tides, etc.). However, as a general
le, try a shallow to deep trolling pattern that pulls baits at-
actively across the top of a wall, edge, curve or drop-off
ey areas patrolled by gamefish). Passes targeting either the
pcurrent or downcurrent (wherever the bait is concentrat-
) side of humps, underwater mountains and deep wrecks
the typical approach before spider-webbing the entire
ructure.

Study a navigational chart to find major structure high-
hts. Areas where curves or drops are in close proximity
e usually very productive, especially when washed by swift
rrents. Structure fishing isn't only reserved for hard bot-
m. Suspended structure is defined as any submerged or
ating masses sustaining bait. These include FADs (fish ag-
egating devices), weedlines and debris. Dolphin anglers,
r example, often run many miles from productive bottom to
eedlines and floating objects for their catches. Juvenile fish
ke sanctuary in the flotsam which, in turn, attract larger
edators. Weedlines and floating debris help narrow down
e search for fish in an open ocean.

Although much more difficult to locate than hard and
spended structure, areas with heavy squid concentrations
n be a good bet. A finely tuned, quality fishfinder is a must.
you're way offshore and signs of life are at a premium, scan
e recorder for bait in the mid and lower water column. Bill-
h, tuna and dolphin rarely stray far from their food and
ckets rich with squid are worthy of attention. Locating
uid boats and longliners can help narrow the search.

The smart angler keeps track of pockets of bait, tem-
erature or color changes and other signs of life enroute to his
imary destination, no matter how insignificant they are.
nce their coordinates are recorded into the loran, they serve
back-ups if the main spot fails to produce.

EEK AT TROLLING TECHNIQUES
AND PATTERNS:

hooling baitfish stay close together for security, the com-
ct size of their masses often confusing predators. Should
ish break stride in a panic or lag behind the group, it's

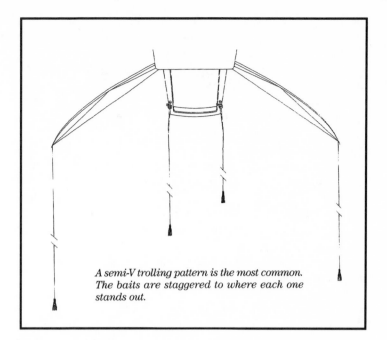

A semi-V trolling pattern is the most common. The baits are staggered to where each one stands out.

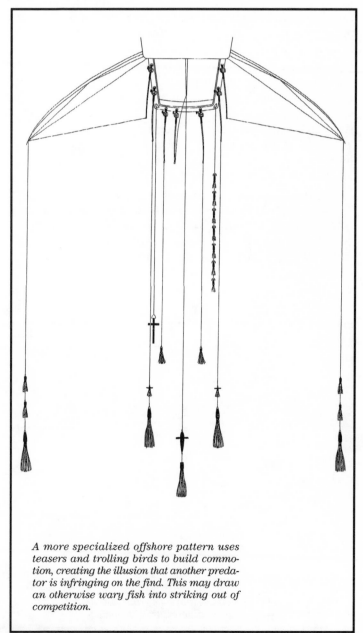

A more specialized offshore pattern uses teasers and trolling birds to build commotion, creating the illusion that another preda- tor is infringing on the find. This may draw an otherwise wary fish into striking out of competition.

probably the one that doesn't go far under the auspices of a threatening gamefish. The objective of a trolling spread is to closely pattern it after a school of bait. Everyone has their own theories on how and where to arrange a spread, stemming from two basic approaches. The first involves the standard running pattern where several similar baits are staggered in a semi-v formation. The forerunners (usually fished off the flat lines just outside of the prop wash) comprise the narrow portion of the spread. Behind them in a wide, staggered formation (from the outriggers) are the remaining baits. Access to a center rigger enables a bait to be fished several yards behind the spread, which can make a difference if fish are leery of the boat. Properly organized the baits appear in a smooth, orderly fashion with enough stagger for each one to stand out.

The second approach uses teasers and trolling birds as attractors, and to create an aura of pandemonium. By building commotion into a spread, the extra sound and vibrations may raise fish on a slow day. In addition, the thrashing of oversized teasers or birds can trigger wary fish into striking by creating the illusion of another predator infringing on their find. There are specialized patterns for different species, but impressive results are often based on individual lures or baits trailing small to medium size birds and as many as three large hookless teasers: one close to the transom, another about three feet in front of and to one side of a flat line bait, and the farthest one (deployed from an outrigger) positioned about three feet ahead of that bait. A larger bird and bait fished well beyond the spread will cover the rear quarter.

Getting a bait or lure to run properly is probably more important than color. It's believed that fish can only distinguish shades, lacking the ability to recognize specific hues. Furthermore, the speeds at which most offshore lures are fished (where they trap air and smoke on their slight descent) make it difficult for a fish to see much more than their commotion and silhouette. Black, purple and blue are popular billfish colors because the darker shades permeate farther through the water column than the reds, the least discernible. However, some match lure colors to the most

Offshore lures run best when fished on the front side of a wa created by the boat's wake. They needn't be pulled at bre neck speeds either. They're at their peak when they gulp air a then dig just beneath the surface for about 15 or 20 feet, leavi a jet-like smoke trail.

abundant baitfish, theorizing that their shades will resemb those that the billfish are presently preying upon (i green/blue if the dolphin are thick, purple/gray with bonit Don't be afraid to add a lure or color that radically stra from the others, where contrasting shades or tracking a gles isolate it. It could prove to be the hottest in the sprea Exactly where and how to run baits or lures depends on s conditions, boat size, trolling speed and the size and type bait. However, skipping baits often perform best when they just breaking water, not being pulled from it, while flat he lures should purge the surface just long enough to trap air b fore embarking on a brief "smoking" sub-surface run. The baits and lure styles troll best between five and 10-kno The heavier, streamlined heads spend most of their time b neath the surface. They're popular on tuna and wahoo a operate best between 10 and 15-knots.

The closest baits are positioned where the prop wa fades into clear water. Many feel that the agitated water he attract fish and that by having a pair of baits nearby can o be beneficial. The remaining baits are staggered and s where they ride attractively through the sea. Be aware th keeping a spread in tune requires constant adjustments. J

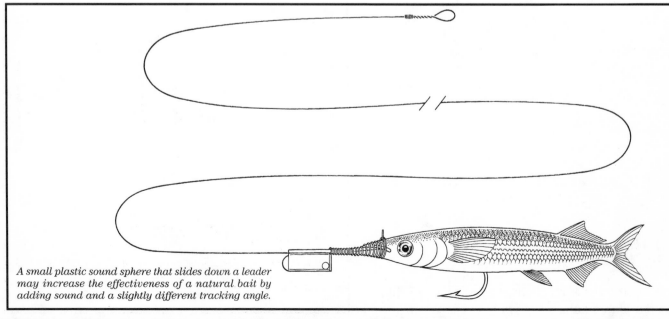

A small plastic sound sphere that slides down a leader may increase the effectiveness of a natural bait by adding sound and a slightly different tracking angle.

because baits are working properly down sea doesn't mean they'll perform as well in another direction. It takes experimentation and a keen eye to counter changing sea conditions. A general rule of thumb, however, is that it's best to fish baits farther back in heavy seas where they're not subject to the sudden lunges of a boat and the whipping of the outriggers. Rough seas also present good a opportunity to fish swimming baits that are more visible under the white caps, and the use of transom clips to reduce the flat lines' angle of entry. Just how many baits can fit into a spread depends upon your boat's set-up. Outriggers with dual bait capabilities (two separate clips and lanyards on each pole) account for a total of four baits, while the two flat lines and a center rigger can inflate that figure by three outfits. Deploying as many baits as possible will increase a boat's fish-ability, providing they're properly rigged and set and there's the man-power to efficiently handle multiple hookups.

HOOKING, FIGHTING, LANDING FISH:

Hook setting techniques vary among the fish sought, bait type and the anglers themselves. However, offshore trolling lures that are traditionally fished with the hard fighting drags are now subject to a unique approach. To enable a fish to gain complete possession of a lure, and hopefully turn away from the boat to set up a better striking angle, drags are engaged only enough to hold the artificials in place. When a fish, such as a marlin or tuna, clobbers the bait, they'll feel little resistance and hang onto the lure longer. The angler advances the drag lever to the strike setting after he's in the chair and ready for battle. The technique closely parallels natural bait fishing and is worth considering if traditional methods are failing.

Fighting a large fish requires teamwork. After the hookup, and about 30-seconds into the trail blazing run, the helmsman will slip the boat out of gear and then concentrate on closing the gap between angler and fish. If an angler is aboard a center console, the boat is spun sideways to enable him to transfer to the bow while still retaining a straight angle on the fish, using the boat's speed and maneuverability to run it down. The initial stages of the battle, where you're trying to get the fish under control, are the most crucial. Letting an excessive amount of line pay behind a wild fish can form a bow, subjecting it to incredible pressure. When in pursuit, avoid the urge to head directly toward the fish, which may not eliminate (and possibly worsen) the bow. Instead, follow the line through the water until you regain a straight attitude.

Your heart and tackle have to be 100 percent into the game. If you're lacking on either, you may never be able to rise to the challenge when that oversize trophy inhales a bait. That's a 754 pound blue marlin at the transom!

Once the fish is under control and sounding, or moving off in an anticipated direction, that's the time to settle down into a give and take battle.

Short, quick pumps are often more effective on a fish that's stubbornly holding in the depths. Each pump may only pay a half-turn on the reel, but the increase in pressure and activity keeps the fish from resting and possibly regaining strength. It's a tough battle and the angler must pace himself. His "breather" comes when the fish is taking line, not when there's an opportunity to gain it. The battle can be grueling all the way to the wire and particularly frustrating when the fish can be seen turning broadside to the current to alleviate some of its pressure. Keep a cool head and don't become discouraged. Hold to your technique, refusing to break stride or do something foolish that can cost you the game.

The final stages are nerve-racking. You've come this far with the trophy and to lose it now would be a painful blow. You're tired and your reflexes aren't what they were when you first took the rod. Pressure mounts on the captain to

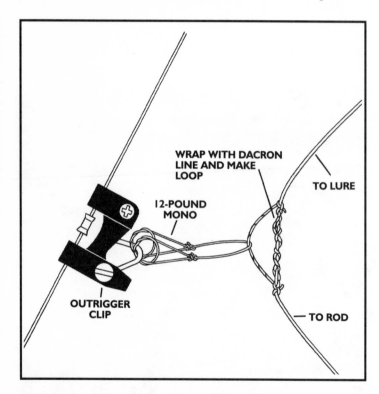

WRAP WITH DACRON
LINE AND MAKE
LOOP

TO LURE

12-POUND
MONO

OUTRIGGER
CLIP

TO ROD

A simple tag-line modification can reduce damage to the fishing line due to the friction and heat produced by slicing through a rubber band. The arrangement requires a 24-inch strand of 12-pound monofilament (loop at both ends), and a Dacron wrap of the same length (with a small loop). The Dacron should be secured to the primary fishing line where the rubber band would normally attach. Match the breaking strength of the Dacron to the actual fishing line for the best fit. Insert both mono loops into a tightened outrigger clip, after running one end through the Dacron eye. That's all there is to it. The slight drop-back is sufficient enough for the fish to turn before the line comes taught, resulting in a better striking angle. The Dacron wrap is tight, yet adjustable to slide along the fishing line when fine tuning a lure's position. The strike will break the light mono, so it pays to have a collection of these "strands" on hand. Experiments with heavier mono (40-pound test) weren't as productive. It's believed that fish that are unsuccessfully hooked may be reluctant to charge a lure again after feeling the excessive pressure.

There's no such thing as a one man band in big game fishing. Landing a trophy requires a good team. Everyone's role shoul. be mentally rehearsed before the boat leaves the dock.

lead the fish to the wireman and to stay alert to counter an. last-second surges. Once the mate takes the leader, back of the drag to give him slack if he needs to move with the fish or if he has to turn it loose. You can always gradually advanc. the drag while the fish is running if the latter occurs, elim. nating the chance of snapping the line when the slack come. tight against a hard drag.

A fish under control and alongside the boat is a beauti. ful sight. It's at this point where the angler must decid. whether to gaff it, or set it free. If he chooses the latter an. the fish is in good condition, remove the hook or clip th. leader close to the fish's mouth. Teamwork is essential in bi. game fishing and everyone's role should be assigned an. played out mentally before the boat clears the inlet.

Becoming good on the offshore grounds requires deter. mination and the ability to learn all you can about its specie. and the latest techniques. Ask questions and don't be afrai. to experiment. One thing offshore fishing isn't is boring. If yo. take your sport seriously and savor its rewards, you'll kee. plenty busy trying to find that "edge" that leads you to a ba. ner day.

continuing trend toward larger boats has incited trailer manufacturers to experiment with various equipment packages to improve the durability, safety and longevity of their products. Whereas a 25-foot boat was considered extremely large for a trailer several years ago, fishing rigs in the 26- to 3-foot range, complete with beams approaching nine feet, are fast becoming a common sight at boat ramps today. Aside from their sheer size, the weight of additional fiberglass, increased fuel capacities and larger or twin power plants require precise trailer adjustments.

Following the advancements of the boating industry, trailers have also become state of the art. Sporting various styles and options, today's trailer market can overwhelm the consumer. Deciding between the two basic designs, float-on or winch-on, poses a problem to most new boat owners.

Before the final choice, a trailer-boater must take into account the range of his outings and the quality of available ramps. If the ramps slope gradually, he might opt for the swift launching/retrieving convenience of a float-on trailer. Conversely, if the ramps are in poor shape, with abrupt drop-offs, or if the boater frequently explores distant fishing haunts, a winch-on design would better serve him.

While quick launching/retrieving is the main advantage of a float-on trailer, its use is limited to quality ramps. Furthermore, the submerging of the frame in salt water usually wreaks havoc on brakes and related equipment. If regular fresh water flushings and general maintenance aren't performed, bearing damage is also possible.

Since most float-ons are constructed with aluminum (some companies produce galvanized steel models), it's usually more cost efficient to replace the entire frame should a section become damaged in an accident. Simply cutting the twisted piece and welding in a new one (typical of steel repairs), isn't feasible.

Other problems associated with float-ons concern the minimum amount of crossmember points supporting a vessel's weight. Combined with the flex of the aluminum over a long range trip, damage to a boat's hull can arise. The better designs feature cross member/poly supports that are strategically positioned every few feet (depending upon the size of the trailer) and fully adjustable side and rear bunks. By evenly distributing and securing a boat's weight over increased support points, the probability of an innate problem should be lessened.

The advantage of the float-on trailer is the demise of the competition. Winch-ons simply take longer at the ramp. However, they can launch most everywhere and, if an owner is careful not to submerge the wheels, brake and bearing life is comparatively increased. Anglers who trailer extensively know that there are many desolate ramps that are best serviced by a winch-on trailer.

THE WEIGHT FACTOR

The most common mistake made after purchasing a trailer is loading it with a boat exceeding the trailer's maximum weight capacity. Overloading results in increased tire wear, bearing failure and, in severe cases, serious accidents. A trailer, regardless of style, must be built according to the vessel's length and weight. When a trailer is custom ordered, manufacturers determine whether its cross members will be straight or angled by the degree of vee on the vessel's transom (not bow). Inboard models have notched crossmembers to permit prop shaft and rudder clearance.

The vessel's loaded weight will also determine the proper trailering equipment. Reputable companies adhere to specific packages based on this information. For example, if the total weight of a boat is 2,000 pounds, a suitable trailer should come with an axle rated for at least 3,000 pounds, 13-inch C-ply tires (1,315 pounds load range per tire) and two five-leaf springs. If a rig weighs in at 2,500 pounds, the same axle should be used, but in conjunction with 14-inch tires (1,710 pounds load range per tire) and two six-leaf springs. Packages

trailer must reflect the range of an owner's outings and the quality of available ramps. A float-on design launches quick and easy, but a winch-on trailer is a better choice where there's an abrupt drop off or a poorly maintained ramp.

are upgraded to the top of the line trailerable boats, with dual axles rated for 7,000 pounds each, four 15-inch D-ply tires (2,370 pounds load range per tire), four six leaf springs and four-wheel braking systems. By underrating the weight capacities of a trailer, one can guard against overloading and extend product life.

THE BARE NECESSITIES

Once the trailer's load capacity is determined, the chore of selecting options begins. With a winch-on trailer, there's a choice between the standard rubber rollers or the more expensive rollers made of polyurethane composition. Rubber rollers have a tendency to develop permanent flat spots if the boat remains parked for a period of time. They can crack or split along the mold mark with age, leaving unattractive markings on the hull. Poly rollers are much more durable, and they recover from flat spotting. As a corrosion preventative, some manufacturers offer stainless steel roller shafts and galvanized axles. Leaf springs can be Dacrotized (an advanced form of zinc plating) to retard rust, as well. Waterproof lights are compulsory. And a walkboard to provide sure footing, while guiding a boat on the trailer, may be a good idea.

Never trust a single safety chain. In addition to the one that will keep a boat on the trailer should the winch give way, run a second chain from the bow eye to the trailer directly below it; it'll prevent the boat from launching onto the trailering vehicle during a sudden stop or impact.

Whether or not the above options are chosen, Bearing Buddies should be included in the budget. These self-encapsulated grease reservoirs continually lubricate wheel bearings, while sealing out water and grit. A proper lubrication level is maintained through center grease fittings. In addition, make certain the trailer fenders have braces capable of supporting a person's weight.

On most trailers accommodating boats up to 21-feet a standard dolly jack is sufficient, but additional support is necessary for heavier equipment. The strains placed by a large boat on standard jacks can split their stand wheels or even collapse the entire unit, prompting a search for a commercial stand with a flat pad that's rated for weights from 5,000 to

10,000 pounds. Make certain your choice provides adequate clearance from your receiver.

POWER PLAY

Selecting the proper winch is another time-consuming yet critical procedure. As in choosing a trailer, the vessel weight should dictate a winch's pulling capacity. Obviously small skiffs can be loaded with an inexpensive manual winch. Ditto for float-ons. However, an electric powered winch becomes a necessity on boats larger than 21 feet. The rated load capacities of most major brand electrical winches will range from 1,000 to 6,000 pounds, on a direct pull. Double line models are equipped with a longer cable and hook, for increasing weight capacity. For example, a unit with a rated load capacity of 4,000 pounds (straight pull) can handle up to 8,000 pounds by doubling back its cable. The boat's retrieval will be half as fast compared to a straight pull, but twice as effective.

Make certain the winch offers a powerful braking system to aid in launching and in securing the boat on the trailer, and that its gears are predominantly weather-safe. It's an integral part of your trailer and should be selected accordingly.

FINE TUNING AND KEEPING IT NEW

The most critical stage of a typical trailer/boat relationship is the final adjustment. The boat should be brought back to the dealer fully loaded for a precise fit. The center and keel rollers, along with any chocks, will be checked for proper height, and realigned if necessary. The trailer's undercarriage will also be offset, until a proper tongue weight is obtained. Most dealers define proper tongue ballast as 12 percent of vessel's weight. Improperly aligned trailers can result in frame and roller damage, increased strains on the winch, fishtailing and damage to the boat.

Proper usage and maintenance will ultimately determine a trailer's longevity. With a winch-on trailer, try to keep the water from reaching the hubs of the rear axle. By doing so you'll minimize bearing and brake problems. By experimenting at the local ramp, you can quickly learn the minimum depth of water required to launch your boat; you'll soon be astonished at how little is really necessary. To prevent damage, always remember to winch the boat off and on slowly. Never unhook the boat, so that it rolls off freely.

After each outing, spray the undercarriage with a soap solution and rinse with fresh water, paying particular attention to springs and brakes. This is especially crucial on float-ons. About every other month, check the electrical connections for signs of corrosion. Take the time to loosen, lubricate and retighten wheel bolts and rollers to prevent freezing. And do not let a year pass without a thorough inspection of brakes and bearings, replacing parts at the slightest hint of corrosion or pitting.

Properly maintaining a trailer requires a fair amount of time. Don't be misled and foolishly bank on the theory that today's trailers are virtually indestructible. Nothing could be further from the truth. By choosing the right trailer for the job and adhering to a strict upkeep schedule, the perceptive boater has already maximized his chances for trouble-free outings.

Vehicles in the 3/4- and 1-ton range are the ticket to safely pulling large scale, trailerable boats.

...hat's wrong with this picture? Absolutely nothing! Putting a ...ist in both sides before tightening a strap reduces vibration, ...eventing wear and tear on its critical stitching and damage ... a boat's finish.

...HOOSING THE RIGHT TRAILERING VEHICLE

...In his quest for the perfect towing vehicle, the sports-...an must set his own criteria. Because he will be concerned ...imarily with trailering, the size and weight of his boat must ...fluence his decision. The buzz phrase here is GROSS COM-...INED WEIGHT RATINGS (GCWR). Often overlooked or ...isunderstood by the boating public, the GCWR of a vehicle ...cludes the combined, loaded weights of the vehicle, boat ...d trailer. It is the guideline that should determine what ...pe of trailering vehicle is compatible with a specific boat, ...e of the least-understood aspects of trailer boating.

Whereas a 25-foot sport fishing boat may look sporty at-...ched to a full scale 4 X 4, chances are the vessel's weight ...r exceeds its GCWR. When you consider that a full-scale 4 ...4 weighs in around 5,500 pounds, that leaves about 4,500 ...unds allotted to the vessel and trailer (based on the vehi-...e's average GCWR of 10,000 pounds). A fully loaded, twin ...owered 25-footer may weigh in excess of 6,000 pounds, ...ith 26 and 27 footers coming in heavier. Trailering these ...ats with vehicles in this GCWR class will result in over-...ading and sever drive train wear. In addition, their short

wheel base (distance between front and rear wheels) won't distribute the weight efficiently, allowing the tonnage to jeopardize handling and overall safety.

DECISIONS, DECISIONS

Lightweight skiffs of up to 18-feet provide the widest range of trailering versatility. Popular towing vehicles for this class of fishing boats include mini 4 X 4's, small pickups and economy vans. Besides a choice between four- and six-cylinder performance, roominess should be a consideration. Will the sportsman adjust comfortably to the limited seating of a pickup, or does the multiple member family require the extra seating of a mini 4 X 4 or a van?

The sportsman must also determine the feasibility of four-wheel drive and/or a towing package. Such a "package" is really a proper combination of engine and gearing (axle ratio). However, most manufacturers offer heavy-duty options, which include springs and shock absorbers, large tires, maximum engine cooling components and, if equipped with an automatic, a heavy-duty auxiliary transmission oil cooler. Because of the limited GCWRs of these smaller trailering vehicles, great care must be taken not to abuse them. They are vulnerable to overloading.

Safely and efficiently trailering boats in the 20- to 23-foot range requires the size and brawn of 1/2-ton pickups and full scale 4 X 4's. This class offers a multitude of power and suspension packages. There's the choice between the payload capabilities of a pickup and the 4 X 4's extra seating.

Full-scale sport vehicles can pull most small and mid-size boats. Never exceed a vehicle's GCWR, which is listed in the owner's manual.

While the pickups have a sharp look to them, the 4 X 4's are a bit classier. Furthermore, their short wheelbases give them a decisive edge in handling.

Depending upon the vessel's weight, there's the choice between the fuel efficiency of a six-cylinder mill (available on most models in this class), the responsiveness of a small eight-cylinder or the full power of a big-block V-8. Diesel power is also available on some models. Then there's the option of four-wheel drive. As any hard core trailer-boater knows, there are times when the additional traction of four-wheel drive is necessary to retrieve a heavy boat from certain ramps, especially at low tide.

Another important consideration is the advantage or disadvantage of a manual transmission. With the quality of today's towing equipment, which includes heavy-duty transmissions and auxiliary coolers, the convenience of an automatic makes for a popular choice. However, if extremely heavy loads are carried by the vehicle, or there are plenty of hills and valleys to round on the way to a ramp, a manual transmission may prove beneficial. By controlling a motor's r.p.m., more torque can be created over a variety of ranges to increase a vehicle's pulling power. The combination of four-wheel drive and a manual transmission, with a granny-gear (an ultra low gear reserved for pulling heavy loads short distances) will get you almost anywhere. The disadvantages are increased wear on the clutch, U-joints and the ring and pinion to a less-than-smooth master of the gears.

The ultimate vehicles for trailering boats over 5,000 pounds are the 3/4- to one-ton capacity models. However, there are needs a trailer-boater should consider before ordering one.

THE MUSCLE FACTOR

Choosing a compatible engine should be a priority. Most range from 301 or 305 cubic inches to big blocks of 454 and 460 cubic inches. Most modern engines are fuel injected and capable of pulling loads near 10,000 pounds. If an angler routinely tows a rig heavier than 5,000 pounds on an interstate with moderate grades, a 350 or 351 cubic inch engine may be desirable, since the torque of a larger block is well worth the extra fuel to master steep inclines or constant stop and go traffic. The lighter side of the big-boat line (under 4,500 pounds) is capably handled by the small V-8 power plants.

Fuel economy isn't a strong point of heavy-duty vehicles, and the difference in fuel savings between the midsize and large V-8s isn't that substantial. Modern diesel engines are gaining in popularity, but despite their fuel savings, boats hauled considerable distances were often "sooted" with spent diesel gasses. Newer models may be better in this regard.

Selecting the proper rear gear ratio will improve fuel mileage. Again, let the size of the boat and the type of driving influence your choice. A "high" rear gearing, such as a 3:08 or a 3:42, is ideal for most interstate situations because it enables the engine to operate efficiently at lower rpm, hence saving quite a bit of fuel. Be aware, however, that such gearing isn't as responsive at slower speeds or in stop and go situations. A rear axle ratio between 3:42 and 3:73 is a good compromise as it provides the necessary low-end torque and operates well at highway speeds, despite pulling more rpm which increases an engines thirst for fuel. A "low" gearing

such as a 4:10 or higher should be reserved strictly for excessive weight loads (above 8,000 pounds) or where low end performance is mandatory. Fuel economy deteriorates rapidly with the lower gears because the engine operates at higher rpm.

SPECIAL SUSPENSION

Truck manufacturers offer special towing packages which include rigid suspensions (heavy duty shocks and springs), extra-capacity radiators (with larger fans or ones with increased pitches), and oversized automatic transmission and engine oil coolers (usually mounted in front of the radiator). Heavy-duty brakes and "E" ply tires (3,042 pound per tire rating) mounted on 16-inch wheels also are available. Although such packages are standard on full-ton models, anyone who routinely trailers a boat should go the extra expense for this vital equipment.

Again, four-wheel drive is another consideration. While the power of a heavy-duty truck is sufficient in drawing a boat from the water, problems may arise from loss of traction on slick ramp surfaces. Vehicles attached to float-on trailers that have to be submerged are especially vulnerable. Going the difference for four-wheel drive can prevent plenty of aggravation and, possibly, a long wait for the tide to get high enough.

THE HITCH

Truck manufacturers shy away from offering heavy-duty factory hitches, citing liability problems. Other than a factory step bumper hitch, rated for light and medium trailers less than 4,000 pounds, you'll have to buy an after-market hitch designed for heavier loads.

Trailer weights exceeding 4,000 pounds require a load distributing hitch platform. The unit bolts to the vehicle frame and distributes the weight evenly between the axle of both units. Load-equalizing hitches come with removable receivers accepting ball diameters of 1-7/8" through 2-5/16". Each restraint chain secured to the trailer with case-hardened bolts should be as strong as the boat's weight. Remember to cross the chains (leaving enough slack for cornering), and insert them from the underside so they can't bounce free. They'll also act as a "catch" and prevent the tongue from dragging if it should come undone. Adjust the boat/trailer so that its tongue accepts about 12 percent of its total weight. Too much weight forward strains drive train, influences "pushing" in a vehicle's handling and promotes premature tire wear. Too much weight aft leads to fishtailing.

COMFORT AND SAFETY

Major mechanical concerns considered, some thought should go into the safety of the driver and crew since trailering a large boat is riskier than driving a car. If possible, select high-back seats that serve as a headrest and can lessen the chance of a head or neck injury in an accident. Furthermore, try to keep enough space, or a headrest, between the rear window of a pickup style vehicle and the operator's seat to minimize contact. Think of your fishing crew as well. If you fish primarily with one or two friends, a single-cab pickup should suffice. Comfortably transporting larger crews or the family will require the additional seating of a pickup with

Consider your crew before buying a trailering vehicle. A pickup may suffice if you usually fish with just one person. Otherwise, the additional seating of an extended cab pickup or a four door model is needed.

n extended cab or a four door model.

Spare belts, hoses, coolant and the necessary tools should be included in a box that travels with the vehicle (aluminum boxes are available that drop down into a pickup bed where they won't interfere with a topper). And as an added safety measure, include several red Cyalume light sticks. Should an electrical short render the tail lights of a trailer or vehicle useless, tape on or insert two light sticks into each housing. This temporary remedy may not buy your way out of a ticket, but at least you'll probably get your rig home safely through the evening hours.

TIE IT DOWN!

In addition to properly adjusting a trailer's bunks, chocks or rollers to accommodate a fully loaded hull, the operator must utilize other safety equipment to insure trouble-free transportation.

Tie-down straps (required by law in some states) prevent the vessel from sliding and/or flipping off the trailer, should the driver swerve suddenly or corner a bit too quickly. There are two main types of restraint straps, the standard tie-down and the heavy-duty ratchet design. The advantages of the latter are twofold. They won't work loose over a period of time and the position of the metal adjustment mechanism is close to a trailer's securing eye. The positional advantage prevents abrasion to outboard motor cowlings from the fastening buckle riding on top, a common problem of standard designs on outboard powered boats.

Vibrations from an improperly adjusted tie-down strap, while traveling, will ultimately damage a boat's gelcoat. Constant agitation can also loosen a belt's critical stitching and chafe its securing hooks, as if a file was taken to them. By simply putting a twist in both sides before tightening the strap, there will be enough tension to retard harmful vibration and any related damage.

A heavy-duty safety chain should be secured to the winch stand, to hold the boat onto the trailer should the winch give way. In addition, a turnbuckle fastened to the trailer directly below and connecting to the bow eye, or a second chain similarly positioned, should be included. This attachment will keep the boat from lunging forward in the event of a sudden stop.

Taking the time to make sure the boat is properly fastened with the above equipment before leaving the driveway is the safe way to start a fishing trip.

KEEPING THEM MOVING

The demand placed on trailering vehicles requires a strict maintenance schedule. Engine oil should be changed every 3,000 miles with a quality brand 10W-40, and transmission oil replaced every 10,000 miles (including that within the torque converter). Belts, hoses, spark plugs and radiator coolant or antifreeze should be changed annually because of intense operating temperatures. Air and fuel filters should be replaced every six months. For added insurance, have a designated dealer periodically check and torque the vehicle's hitch and vital trailer connections (tongue, surge brakes, restraint chains, etc.). It becomes time consuming and a little expensive, but staying on top of your equipment is a necessary safety measure.

TAKE COVER

Custom tailored boat covers, which protect fiberglass from the elements when the boat's at rest, are advantageous on long journeys as well.

Boat covers can eliminate lengthy washdowns caused by a build-up of road grit and bugs. This is especially true in southern states where the summer love-bug season makes its presence known on the windows and grills of highway vehicles. Providing they are secured tightly with no large openings, boating accessories and tackle can be kept under cover during a coffee break and/or an overnight stay. The burden of locking gear into the truck or hustling it into a hotel room is eliminated.

Acrylic, a lightweight and durable fabric, is a prime cover material. Aside from its strength, it has the ability to breathe and keep out moisture. It's less susceptible to rot and lasts about three times longer than treated canvas.

A cover should be designed for an ultra-tight fit, with reinforced corners and points. Any sags will cause it to whip at high speeds and puddles can form, should it rain. A full-length cover that runs down over a boat's chine is an ideal choice for trailering. Although it costs more, there will be less chance of it catching wind on the highway. They also can be tailored to specifically fit around a T-top.

A quality cover comes with an adjustable tie strap, zippers or grommets to tie down with. On extremely long hauls, tying additional rope restraints from the grommets to the trailer is recommended. However, a sponge or towel taped to the portion of the rope making contact with the hull is necessary to prevent chafing.

When launching a rig, covers can be folded and stored inside most towing vehicles. While on the boat, they can be kept clean by simply spraying with a mild soap and rinsing.

A SOLID CONNECTION

With the amount of money invested in a quality boat, plus the ever increasing premiums of both vessel and vehicle, it's best to spring for a quality trailer hitch and be confident that your pride and joy will follow you home after each trip. Don't take a chance on a cheap setup, and have your rig possibly end up in the boondocks, or worse yet, in the highway's head-on lane.

As a rule, a bumper hitch is adequate for loads up to 2,000 pounds, with no more than 200 pounds of tongue weight (Class I). Trailers in excess of 2,000 pounds (Class II-IV) should be attached to a load-equalizing hitch. The advantage of a load equalizer is that it is bolted to the vehicle's frame, distributing equally the weight of the trailer and towing vehicle between the axles of both units. Some step-type rear bumpers on heavy-duty pickups appear ultra strong. However, don't be misled and utilize a bumper hitch on a trailer exceeding a Class I rating. You'd be surprised how quickly they can work loose.

Load equalizing hitches come with removable receivers that can accommodate ball diameters of 1-7/8 to 2-5/16 inches. After each use, remove the receiver and store it in the back of the towing rig to prevent theft (and they do have an uncanny knack of disappearing!). As an added safety feature, load equalizing hitches provide hook retainers for safety chains.

All trailers should come with two heavy-duty chains bolted to the tongue. If the trailer has surge brakes, a third chain should be attached to the auxiliary brake handle located on the tongue. In the unlikely event that the trailer departs from the ball, or the receiver comes free, the crossed safety restraints would catch the tongue and keep the trailer in line behind the vehicle. The surge emergency handle is activated on a trailer with brakes, hopefully stopping it before extensive damage occurs. Make certain to cross the chains under the trailer's tongue, leaving enough slack for cornering. Never attach them to the bumper. As an added safety measure, lock the trailer's tongue onto the ball.

Required maintenance of load equalizing hitches involves inspecting the bolts periodically for tightness, and lubricating the ball and receiver with a light spray lubricant after each use.

PREPARE FOR THE WORST

Although we don't care to think about it, sooner or later trailer-boaters end up on the roadside with an untimely problem. Preparation and foresight can usually minimize the headaches of a mechanical misfortune.

The long distance traveler must stock his towing vehicle with an array of parts and tools to cover common trailering problems, if he has any intention of salvaging a fishing trip. The proximity of the tires on a dual axle trailer should require two spares. If debris such as shattered glass is run over by one tire, it will also be hit by the second wheel in line. Most trailers provide enough forward space to mount and lock spare tires. If space is limited, mount one tire forward and store the other in the back of the towing vehicle. And remember, truck and auto spares generally don't fit trailers.

Because wheel bearing failure is a potential threat, the prepared boater always keeps a complete hub assembly (pre-packed bearings with grease, seals and lug nuts) in a plastic container within the towing vehicle. With an adequate floor jack, capable of lifting the trailer from under the axle, and the proper tools (wrench, screwdriver and hammer), bad bearings can be replaced in short order.

In case an electrical winch fails, it's imperative that a spare handle is packed away. An increasing number of trailer owners carry a spare, relatively cheap electrical winch (with an appropriate power cord and alligator clamps), to eliminate the physical strain of manually loading a boat on the trailer. Should a problem arise with the main unit, the spare can be bolted onto the stand and put into action within minutes.

The tow vehicle itself may need spare parts, such as belts, radiator hoses, etc., as well as several gallons of coolant and water. Also included should be a clear siphoning hose about 15 feet in length. Thanks to the internal oil/fuel mixing capabilities of most late model outboards, the trailer-boater needn't be as concerned with running out of fuel as in years past. Should a situation require it, the boater can draw pure gasoline from the boat's tank, directing it into the vehicle's tank.

Aside from supporting a vehicle at the boat ramp, chocks can provide a jack with extra leverage for raising both vehicle and trailer. A few chocks of various sizes should be kept handy. Other items that might prove useful are a tire gauge, extra lightbulbs for the trailer, tie wraps in the event winch's power cord or trailer wiring needs to be secured to its frame, a fire extinguisher inside the vehicle, a flashlight and a drop light with battery clamps in case nighttime repairs are necessary.

While the average boater who travels just a few miles to the local ramp and back may have trouble justifying the expense of such surplus equipment, the trailer-boater can't afford to be without it. By wisely investing in spare parts and tools, he'll reduce the chance of seeing his fishing trip end up on the business end of a wrecker.

CHAPTER 14 FINDING FISH

The most successful technique for locating fish starts with elimination. Once one develops an understanding of the habits and habitat of the quarry, the first stage in the process falls into place. You have a fair idea where the fish won't be. The key lies in narrowing the search area through continuous updating by weeding out spots that won't produce. Experience might show that the species you want to catch will avoid a specific habitat on a given stage of the tide, time of day, or month of the year.

Being creatures of habit, fish tend to frequent particular areas on a regular basis for extended periods. That helps to narrow the search area. Even without advanced knowledge, a systematic approach tailored to testing the various possibilities still makes sense.

Bass fishermen came up with the word pattern to describe the behavior of some fish at a given time. Several patterns may be in effect simultaneously, but the goal centers on uncovering only one. Use whatever experience you have to rank the various options. If necessary, write them down and number them in order of priority. Then, begin with the most promising and work right down the list. You are trying to eliminate possibilities, so stay alert to signs and signals that could give you the needed clue.

Professional guides may seem like magicians at times, but they really aren't. These skippers know a plethora of spots where the species they seek could be. Based on factors such as today's conditions, where the fish were yesterday, reports from colleagues, and other data, they establish a game plan. If they find fish at the first stop, it's marvelous. If they don't, these pros have eliminated one option and quickly shift to the second.

READING WATER

Reading water ranks as a learned skill. Beginners fail to find the technique obvious or basic. The untrained eye struggles to discern any change in the water, viewing the surface of ocean or estuary as uniform patterns of waves or ripples. Pay your dues and you begin to distinguish subtle differences in color, currents, depths, and temperature. Certain signals catch one's attention whether or not an angler had ever seen the area before.

Fish seek comfort in terms of water temperature, edges, food supply, and water quality. Signs of life head the list in any search pattern. An abundance of sea birds or wading birds indicates food is present. One respected captain notes that birds are better fishers than he is, so he bows to their knowledge. Find these feathered friends and you may have discovered fish.

Schools of bait on the surface, flying fish taking off in front of the boat, or even the single dimples of some forage species make an area interesting. You might actually spot a gamefish or two cruising on the surface, breaking water, swirling, waking, or doing something to give their position away. On the shallow flats, sharks and rays often serve as indicators that more desirable species may be present.

The sea gives many hints as to the whereabouts of its inhabitants. Schools of bait or diving birds, for example, usually mean fish.

Alertness becomes critical. Your eyes must scan the water from your feet to the horizon just as search radar never stops sweeping. Concentration shares the spotlight. Finding fish translates into a mental exercise as much as a physical one. What your eyes see has to trigger a response in the brain.

WATER COLOR

Color ranks as the primary key in reading water. A fundamental change from greenish hues to deep blue occurs as you journey seaward aboard a boat. Veteran anglers seldom touch the throttles or change course until they cross this line of demarcation. Dolphin, billfish, and other species that prefer blue water will be beyond this point. Stopping short of the color shift without good reason usually results in wasted time.

Don't overlook the value of color on the inshore grounds. Water pouring out of an inlet on falling tide may be dirty, forcing the fish to work the zone where the dirty water meets the clean. That's where they have a better chance of picking off forage species being swept seaward by the current.

A specific area of an estuary could be dingy, reducing visibility and perhaps driving fish toward cleaner surroundings. Make it a practice to note water quality in terms of coloration and compare it to nearby waters. You should also be aware of how the water looks on this outing compared to previous trips Anything out of the ordinary usually produces different results.

Under normal conditions, color provides visual clues to the depth. As the water gets darker, it becomes deeper. The boundaries of a channel stand out from the shallower water on either side if you look closely. Isolated pockets of a darker hue may be deeper holes spread over skinnier water. Sometimes, the reverse is true. On a grass flat, deeper holes may be devoid of any growth, leaving only white sand. Known as potholes, they appear lighter in color than the surrounding terrain. Once you identify the first one, spotting similar structure is easy.

There are always exceptions. Mullet rooting in the bottom stir up sediment forming what anglers call a mullet mud. During chilly weather, this discolored water absorbs and holds the heat. Predators know that it will be more tolerable for them and that's where the food supply happens to be.

GAINING AN EDGE

Any animal gravitates to an edge and fish follow a similar pattern. Consider an edge to be a transitional zone where a change takes place. A different condition exists on either side of the line. The most vivid example focuses on a color change. It may be blue and clear on one side, green and dingy on the other. Working this sector could produce results. The tendency is to stay on the blue side or, in the case of dirty and clean water, on the clean side. If you don't raise fish within a

short period, try the other side. It may not seem logical, b it could produce results.

Almost any difference constitutes an edge. You have or where a current starts. The bottom may go from rock to sar or mud to grass. The inshore or offshore rims of a reefline f into the category. Where water temperature changes, yo have a different type of edge. Find an edge and you will prob ably locate fish.

WATER DEPTH

If you could ask a successful angler a single questic about where he caught fish, what would you want to know Assuming he won't mark the precise spot on a chart for you the next most valuable information is simply the water dept Once you know that, you can figure out places to fish.

No one really understands the mechanics of a water co umn or why a fish selects a particular depth. What we know is that there are days when a certain species will opt f a given depth either inshore or offshore. Bluewater angle would love to know the productive depth. If you knew th water depth for summer flounder (fluke) on the insho grounds, it wouldn't take long to find a concentration.

For those who fish rivers or creeks, the outside banks a deeper because the current sweeps against them and carve them out. In the northeast, jetties jutting out into the se usually have a deeper pocket on the southeast corner with secondary pocket on the northeast corner. The sweep of t sea digs them out and fish often hold right there close to t rocks.

Beaches have deeper sloughs that run parallel to t sand and cuts between the bars that serve as highways deep water. Surfcasters know that fish use these as highway to move in and out and then to search for food.

WATER TEMPERATURE

Water temperature is still the single most importal factor in determining where fish will be at any given m

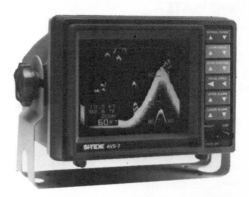

Water temperature is still the single most important factor in determining where fish will be. Quality fishfinders and cole sounders prominently display these temperatures.

A rip as pronounced as this could produce some outstanding catches. Such a transitional zone can be caused by the convergence of different currents or one that washes against a dropoff or hump.

ment. It may be one of the hidden factors explaining wh fish prefer a specific depth. Many species can detect change as minute as 1/100th of a degree. If the temperature reac only one degree warmer or cooler than the surrounding w ter, that's enough to make a difference. The fish, of cours could be on one side of the edge or the other.

A sudden chilling of the water by a northeaster in the summer usually sends bluefish scurrying for more comfortable surroundings, while summer flounder quickly bury in the mud. Even in the tropics, water temperature makes a significant difference. A thermometer proves to be one of the most valuable items aboard a boat or in a tackle box. Serious fishermen won't run a boat without one and they monitor it constantly. If you don't have one, try putting your hand in the water. It may lack the sensitivity of an instrument, but you may gain a clue.

Canyon runners know all about warm water gyres that break off from the Gulf Stream. Temperature changes along the edge of the Continental Shelf share the same importance as they do inshore. Each species has a temperature tolerance range and a comfort zone. They may exceed the parameters of their comfort zone from time to time, but they are physically unable to survive very long in water warmer or colder than their tolerance range. Fish are cold-blooded which means that water temperature affects their bodily functions. That's why they become sluggish when the water gets too cold and have problems when it gets too warm.

At the bottom of their tolerance, fish try to exert much less energy in feeding. Don't expect a striped bass in marginal water to chase a cha-chaing surface plug and crash it with summertime fury.

FLOWING WATER

In the marine environment, water constantly moves. Fish relate and adjust to tidal currents, ocean currents, and any other flow of water. To remain relatively stationary, they must face into the current. Instinctively, every species attempts to reduce the expenditure of energy by taking up station along the edge of the flow, just outside it where they can dart in to grab a tidbit, close to the bottom where the water's force is reduced, or near an obstruction.

If you can find a spot or two where the topography causes a neck or funnel effect, check those places first. Another starting point occurs where two currents join. It may be a feeder stream entering the primary flow or a Y coming together. By narrowing the search pattern, you follow the doctrine of elimination, concentrating on the most likely places first.

Inlets fit this category, because they funnel the water from an estuary into the ocean. Usually, they prove more effective on outgoing water. Fish often stack up and wait for the current to carry bait seaward. Check the edges of the primary current and get baits down near the bottom where the flow isn't quite as strong. If there is a bridge, fish should take up station in front of or behind the structural supports. Both locations create dead spots where current is minimal.

Major ocean currents flow like a river, pulling surface water as they move. Replacement water comes from the depths through a process known as upwelling. As this colder water rises from the bottom, the sun causes plankton to bloom. Forage species feed on the plankton and gamefish prowl the edges searching for the little guys.

A junction occurs where one body of water enters another. Fish know that food will be carried down the tribu-

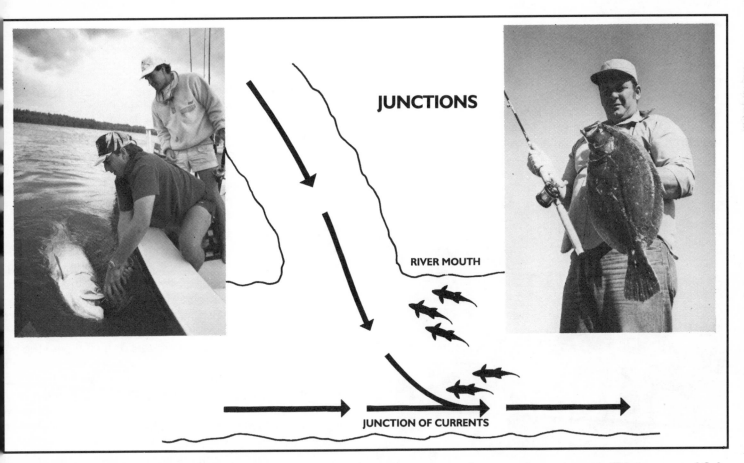

The junction of currents, such as a feeder stream entering a primary channel, are always good spots to work. This tarpon and fluke are classic examples of inshore fish that gravitate toward these systems.

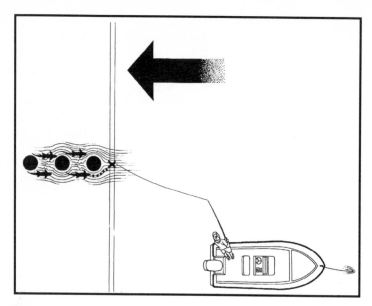

Pilings and bridges are notorious for holding fish. Work a bait or lure around the dead spots both uptide and downcurrent of the structure.

tary into the main estuary. You can expect to find them waiting at the mouth. In some places, this may be a tidal situation. Where tiny creeks empty into a bay or river, baitfish may seek a sanctuary in the shallows during rising water. At the bottom of the tide, there may not be enough water for the forage species. Predators line up and wait for the smaller fish to enter the main body.

THE SEA FLOOR

Seasoned anglers monitor their depth sounders continuously. Any rise in the sea floor is worth investigating. Fish hang around humps, lumps, mounds, rocks, reefs, wrecks, and anything else that sticks up from the bottom. In some areas, it does not take a very significant rise to hold quantities of fish. Any obstruction interrupts the flow of water, causing the current to sweep around it or over the top. Bait orients

Bottom structure contains bait and gamefish. Use a fishfinder to scan the ocean's floor and lead you to fish like this grouper.

to this type of habitat and gamefish linger here.

When you spot a sea turtle on the surface, scout the area carefully using a depth sounder. Invariably, you'll find some type of obstruction or rise on the bottom. You may see fish on the surface in open water. They, too, may be telegraphing the message that you have found structure. Any

When a tidal current is flowing, look for fish to hang out in the dead spot uptide of a wreck or other piece of structure as well as on the downcurrent side. Larger bottom dwellers prefer the drop-offs on the sides of a wreck or mound, frequently hovering above it when the current subsides. Don't overlook the potential of inshore or shallow wrecks and structure, and also any pelagics which may appear in the upper water column.

sighting on the surface begs a check with a depth sounder.

Once you locate a rise in the sea floor, investigate the area thoroughly. Bottom species will hold tight to the structure, but pelagics tend to roam. Depending on the amount of current, they could stray farther from the mark than you might suspect. It's equally important to work the various sides of any rise. The primary concentration of fish could be on either the upcurrent or downcurrent edge.

SLOPES AND DROPOFFS

Put this feature high on your list of prime spots. Fish love dropoffs. Predators lurk beneath their victims, preferring to attack upward. You'll find the heavyweights staggered down the dropoff or patrolling just off the edge. When you locate this habitat, work your baits or lures from shallow to deep. If that doesn't produce, reverse the direction.

A slope is simply a more gradual dropoff where the bottom tapers into deeper water. This is the perfect terrain to discover holding depth for some species. Walk a bait down the slope from shallow to deep. Slopes loom even more prominently when they are associated with a point. By studying a chart, you can often locate these places even if you have never fished the area before.

Any transitional zone is worth checking out. Dropoffs and slopes meet the requirements. They also create edges and that's where fish will be.

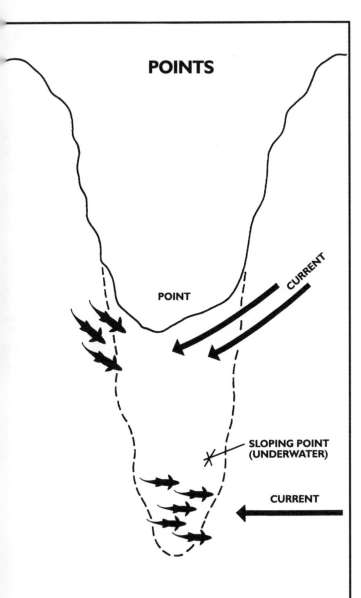

POINTS

POINT

CURRENT

CURRENT

**SLOPING POINT
(UNDERWATER)**

Drop-offs and points all attract gamefish consistently because they offer predators an opportunity to catch an easy meal. Presenting a lure or bait in a natural manner is the key to success.

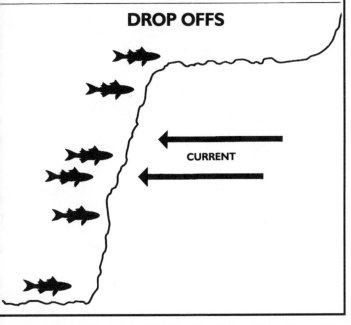

DROP OFFS

CURRENT

POINTS AND POCKETS

Points offer predators the perfect place to ambush their prey. The jutting land mass provides concealment, excellent visibility, and a sanctuary out of the current. Usually, water flows past one side of a point, creating a lee on the backside. Your bait should sweep through the area in a natural manner, approaching with the current. Cast beyond where you expect the fish to be and then retrieve with the flow of water. If anybody is home, the rod should scribe the traditional arc very quickly.

If you see a point of land, you can be reasonably certain that the same configuration continues underwater. Points may be shallow, but if the land above the surface drops, expect the fall to continue below the waterline. Points with access to deep water frequently rank as top spots.

Certain species lie or cruise well back in shoreline pockets, following the contour of the land mass. They know that baitfish tend to push into the very shallow water to escape the gaping jaws of a huskier critter. Pockets that have a thin lip and then drop off are even better. Forage species stay on the rim, while predators wait for an errant tidbit to venture over the edge.

If the pocket is surrounded by cover, expect the fish to be lurking where they are concealed. That gives them a good view of the open water in the pocket and they can dart out to grab anything that moves.

SHORELINES

Casting or trolling a shoreline can be fun and productive. Exploring this type of habitat at random may not produce the desired results. A better approach centers on identifying features and fishing them carefully. You already know about points and pockets, but there are other configurations that should catch your eye.

Make every cast count. Rather than tossing without thought, select the precise spot you would expect to find a fish and then make the perfect presentation. Every time you cast, you should pick out a feature and fish it. To reach certain spots, you must wait for a window as the boat moves. Calculate the angles in advance so that you are ready to get a bait into the best looking places. You may have to wait a moment or two between casts, but you'll fish a shoreline more effectively if you engineer every effort.

When a wind is blowing, the windward shoreline could hold more fish than a lee shore. It's difficult to fish, but worth the time. The wind could drive bait against the shore and that's where the predators will be. In some estuaries, the windward side provides fish with more oxygen.

A REMINDER

Finding fish, like any research, focuses on elimination. By determining where the fish won't be, you have a better chance of uncovering their present location. The key lies in making each decision based on valid reasoning. Before you start, try to eliminate as much water as possible. Then, concentrate your attention on the places that should hold fish. Start with your best bet and work down the list. As long as you keep eliminating options, you should increase your effectiveness. If it works for professional captains, it should help you catch fish.

Once you develop an understanding of the habits and habitat of your favorite fish, finding them won't be that big of a challenge.

**THE SALT WATER SPORTSMAN SEMINAR SERIES
IS MADE POSSIBLE THROUGH THE COOPERATION
OF THE FOLLOWING SPONSORS:**

SI-TEX MARINE ELECTRONICS

ANDE MONOFILAMENT

CANNON DOWNRIGGERS

PENN REELS

EAGLE CLAW FISH HOOKS

DELCO-VOYAGER

THE ISLANDS OF THE BAHAMAS

MAKO MARINE INTERNATIONAL

RAPALA BY NORMARK

JOHNSON/EVINRUDE OUTBOARDS

CAPT. HARRY'S

SPERRY TOP-SIDER

VOLVO PENTA

AMERICAN AIRLINES
AMERICAN EAGLE

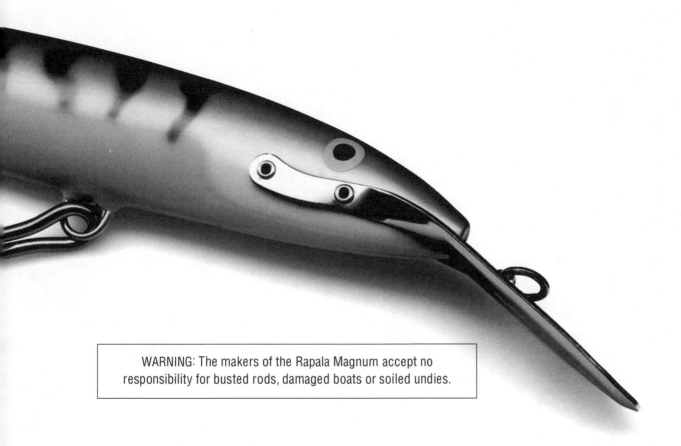

WARNING: The makers of the Rapala Magnum accept no responsibility for busted rods, damaged boats or soiled undies.

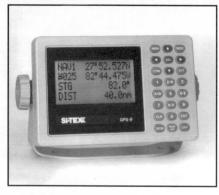

GPS works in both Lat/Lon coordinates and Loran TD's.

Advanced continuous-tracking *MaxView* receiver of the **SI-TEX GPS-9** processes data from up to 11 GPS satellites for highly accurate position updates every second • Differential-ready receiver automatically displays your position at turn-on • Position data can be entered and displayed in both Lat/Lon coordinates and Loran TD's • Easy-to-use softkey controls and on-screen operating menus • Selectable displays of boat speed and heading plus the bearing, distance and time to next waypoint • XTE, CDI courseline steering guidance • 130 waypoints, ten reversible routes and 20 instant-positions • MOB mode • Flush-mount kit available • Case size: 5"H x 7.5"W x 2.6"D

Bluewater LCD depth sounder/ plotter with GPS option.

Depth sounder portion of **SI-TEX LCS-300** has 2000 watts of peak power and seven ranges to 640' • Auto Range, Auto Gain, A-Scope, Zoom and Bottom Lock Expansion * Keel alarm and seven-level fish alarm • Eleven plotter scales to 120 NM with Auto Scale Control • Exclusive *ChartDraw* feature lets you create and store your own outline maps and charts • Position data input from optional GPS-10 makes it a full-function GPS plotter • 100 WPT's, 250 event marks • Case size: 8.5"H x 8.2"W x 2.8"D

GPS-10

Six-inch color video sounder with speed, temp and log.

The **SI-TEX CVS-106** offers top-notch performance and versatility in a compact video sounder • Brilliant eight-color display • Eight basic ranges to 1280 feet with Automatic Range Control • Power output of 200 watts RMS (1600 watts peak-to-peak) • Shallow/ deep water and multi-level fish alarms • STC • Instant Zoom • Digital readouts of bottom depth, surface water temperature, boat speed and distance traveled • Position display with input from external nav-sensor via NMEA 0183 interface • Big number display for navigation • Available 50, 120 and 200 kHz • Flush-mount kit available • Case size: 6.7"H x 7.5"W x 10"D

A complete line of quality marine electronics with top-notch performance and high reliability at affordable prices.

For complete information, write SI-TEX, 11001 Roosevelt Blvd., Suite 800, St. Petersburg, FL 33716 or Call Customer Service Center: (813) 576-5734

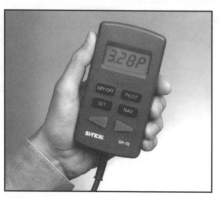

World's most affordable quality marine VHF with programmable memory scan.

The **SI-TEX Compact 66** is the smallest fixed-mount VHF marine radio you can install on your boat. Yet it transmits the full legal limit of 25 watts • One watt selectable for in-harbor communications • Low-priced little powerhouse mounts in tight little places where nothing else seems to fit • Programmable Memory Scan for any desired number of most frequently used channels • Touch-key control of channel selection, emergency channel 16 override and HI/LOW power selection • Five-minute time-out feature to prevent open-mike frequency blocks • External output for remote speaker • Flush-mount bracket available • Case size: 2"H x 5.5"W x 6.25"D

Autopilot for outboard, inboard and sterndrive boats.

The **SI-TEX SP-70** Autopilot offers freedom-from-the-wheel on most outboard, inboard and sterndrive power boats with hydraulic steering systems • Waterproof control unit can be used as a fixed-mount control or quickly and easily removed from bracket and used as a handheld portable • Additional steering stations are easily added with optional plug-in connectors • Backlit LCD display of course, rudder angle and operating mode • Automatic trim control • Ten selectable levels of rudder sensitivity • Loran/GPS interface for precise waypoint navigation • System can be used with solenoid valves • 10—40V DC • Control Unit case size: 5.2"H x 2.8"W x 1"D

Micro-sized LCD radar displays position of target echoes.

The waterproof T-150 in slim, trim case easily fits most any size boat. • Exclusive Dual IF Bandwidths for increased sensitivity • Non-glare 7" super-twist display for crystal-clear clarity • 12 ranges to 16 NM • Adjustable VRM and EBL plus zoom and on screen trail plotting • 12" radome antenna is smallest and lightest on the market • Position-Pick-Off (PPO) control displays position of on-screen targets via NMEA 0812/0813 interface • System includes radome antenna, display cover, plus carrying case • Case size: 7.2" H x 7.6" W x 1.9"D

ABOUT THE SPONSORS

SALT WATER SPORTSMAN: Established nearly a half century ago by Hugh Gray, Tap Tapply, and Ollie Rodman as a New England marine fishing journal, *Salt Water Sportsman* has grown from its original four pages to an international magazine aimed at today's serious salt water sport fisherman. Cuttyhunk line, Vom Hofe star drag reels, and split bamboo or hardwood rods were the standard when that first issue captured the attention of anglers. It was targeted to help them improve their skills and keep up-to-date on new trends in tackle and technique. That trust has never changed.

Following World War II, thousands of returning service personnel flocked to the edge of the sea. *Salt Water Sportsman* was there to chronicle all the improvements in tackle, boats, and fishing methods. Expert anglers such as Hal Lyman, Frank Woolner, Rip Cunningham, Spider Andresen, and Barry Gibson joined its staff. The magazine soon developed a reputation as the authority on this growing sport.

Salt Water Sportsman's philosophy and dedication to the reader haven't changed. Feature stories stress the how-to, where-to aspects with emphasis on conservation. Special sections and monthly departments cover boat selection and maintenance, news items and new products, electronics, engines, vehicles, building and repairing tackle and gear, and regional fishing reports written monthly by local experts.

Editor Emeritus Frank Woolner said it best when he penned, "Take it or leave it, we are SWS as Rodman, Tapply and Gray wanted it to be. Our hero is the man on the beach, the pier, or out on the deep blue." That's the way things will always be at *Salt Water Sportsman.* Count on it!

WITH GREAT PRIDE, WE PRESENT OUR SEMINAR SERIES NATIONAL FACULTY:

GEORGE POVEROMO

RIP CUNNINGHAM   **BARRY GIBSON**   **SPIDER ANDRESEN**   **MARK SOSIN**

AND PROUDLY RECOGNIZE THE FOLLOWING COMPANIES FOR THEIR CONTINUED SUPPORT...

DELCO VOYAGER BATTERIES

Seventeen years ago, automobile owners hailed the introduction of maintenance-free batteries by the Delco Remy Division of General Motors as a major breakthrough. In 1981, the first Delco Voyager tailored specifically for marine and RV use set the modern day standard.

Capable of an extraordinary number of charge/discharge cycles, Delco Voyager deep cycle batteries provide the necessary starting power for boats and RVs while handling all of the electrical accessories. The maintenance-free, envelope construction prevents internal shorting and improves vibration durability. An expanded wrought lead-calcium grid adds strength and resists corrosion, overcharge, gassing, water usage, self-discharge, and thermal runaway.

Delco batteries feature an exclusive liquid-gas separator which prevents minute electrolyte losses. There is a permanent flame arrestor to reduce the risk of accidental explosion, and a state-of-charge monitor. All components are sealed in a lightweight, high-impact, polypropylene case. As an industry leader, Delco Voyager builds top quality batteries engineered to handle the toughest assignments.

In addition to being a proud sponsor of the Salt Water Sportsman National Seminar Series, Delco Voyager also supports Southern Saltwater – Saltwater Trails, B.A.S.S., Bass'N Gal, OWAA, AFTMA, and NMMA.

ANDE LINE

Ande has been supplying monofilament fishing lines to anglers of the world for over 25 years. Their main goal centers on selling the finest monofilament at the most reasonable price. Currently, Ande line users hold over 350 I.G.F.A. World Records, demonstrating the quality and reliability built into every yard and every pound of Premium, Super Soft, and Tournament lines.

Premium Monofilament is the first choice among countless anglers. Available in clear, pink, dark green, and gun metal in tests from 2 to 700 pounds, it is medium soft with excellent tensile and knot strength. Abrasion resistance is exceptional. Tournament Monofilament is pre-tested to break under the recognized line classes for world records and tournaments. It is made in green and tests from 2 to 130 pounds.

Super Soft (2 to 20 pound test) has a slightly smaller diameter and is made for the light tackle caster. Its lack of memory characteristic of most monofilament makes it ideal for those who use bait casting and spinning tackle.

Although they sell line to catch fish, they also encourage anglers everywhere to release what they don't need for their own table. To foster this concept, they have three release programs: the Ande Junior Fishing Tournament, the Master Angler Release Club, and the new Muskie Release Program. Ande is particularly pleased to be part of the Salt Water Sportsman National Seminar Series.

If you would like more information on their release programs, write Ande at 1310 53rd Street, West Palm Beach, Florida 33407.

CANNON/S&K PRODUCTS, INC.

The rebirth of Great Lakes sportfishing created a strong business opportunity for Jim Swinehart and Jack King. The two men worked with determination and perseverance to improve the design and performance of downriggers, culminating in the founding of Cannon/S&K Products in 1979.

Their tireless efforts helped to revolutionize the sport through the concept and technique of controlled-depth fishing. Ed Sutton added his marketing flair to the business and engineering expertise of the founders, quickly propelling Cannon to the number one spot in the industry.

Armstrong International of Three Rivers, Michigan purchased Cannon in 1985, further strengthening Cannon's position and tradition of product innovation. The company currently manufactures and markets a complete line of downriggers for every boat, budget, and body of water. The Marlin Series takes on salt water, the Great Lakes Series is targeted for large lakes and reservoirs, and the Econo Series for smaller boats is designed for inland lakes and rivers. The extensive line includes manual, electric, and computerized models with memory, plus the tough, inexpensive Mini-Troll as an introductory model for controlled-depth fishing.

Other Cannon products include the Helmsman remote-control boat steering system; the Plane-R-Series for side planer trolling; the Speed-N-Temp to read trolling speed, surface water temperature, and temperature at the lure; the Excitor for flatline trolling and jigging; and the Pow-R-Pak, a portable 12V battery pack for downriggers and other marine electronics.

NORMARK CORPORATION ... Dedicated to all of our Loyal Customers

This is a message of *sincere thanks* from all of us who manufacture and distribute Rapala lures to you – the legion of successful anglers whose loyalty has made the "Rapala" name a standard of excellence.

You, more than anyone else, know that Rapalas have met with "unrivaled success" in lakes, streams, rivers and oceans around the world since their introduction some five decades ago.

Although Rapala's success lies in "the secret" discovered by one dedicated angler, Lauri Rapala, in his native Finland during the darkest days of the Great Depression, his successors have listened attentively to you, the fisherman, answering your increasingly special needs with a family of Rapalas geared to your angling needs.

We have said it before, and now we say it again: There will never be any compromise of quality in the production of Rapala lures. There will never be any short-cuts in material or workmanship. Each lure will always be "hand-tested" before shipment to make certain that "the secret" of Lauri Rapala – that lifelike swimming action – is embodied in every lure bearing the Rapala name.

You can always be sure of a Rapala lure – a pledge from Lauri's three sons, Ensio, Risto and Esko Rapala, and from all of us at Normark Corporation, the exclusive distributors of Rapala – "The Lure That Fish Can't Pass Up."

SPERRY TOP-SIDER

In the winter of 1935, Paul Sperry, an avid yachtsman, had been working to develop a skid resistant, rubber-soled shoe to wear on his yacht. At that time, boating shoes were made of canvas uppers attached to either crepe rubber soles or rope soles. Neither option satisfied the demand for superior traction.

One morning, while walking his cocker spaniel, Sperry noticed his pet's incredible sense of balance and stability on the frozen pavement. Sperry examined the bottom of Prince's paw and found a pattern of deep, wave-like grooves. Using a razor blade, Sperry reproduced this pattern on a piece of crepe rubber and attached it to a pair of ordinary canvas sneakers. After testing his invention, he and the members of his crew found it gave near-perfect adhesion on wet, slippery decks.

Since then, Sperry has expanded its line of performance boating shoes to include a complete array of marine performance products designed for the challenges of the high seas. The SB 770, launched in Spring 1995 is the latest development in high performance boat shoes. The shoe was designed jointly with New Balance and combines boat shoe grip performance with cross trainer comfort and fit.

The Sperry Top-Sider name still conjures images of the sea, and the *original* boat shoe company is proud of its marine heritage. The brands ties to the marine life continue, as Sperry Top-Sider will again support The Billfish Foundation, The *Salt Water Sportsman* Seminar Series, and several tournaments such as the White Marlin Open, the Mid-Atlantic $500,000, the Ft. Lauderdale Billfish Tournament, and many other marine related events and organizations.

SI-TEX MARINE ELECTRONICS

With one of the most comprehensive lines of marine electronic products available, SI-TEX offers the serious saltwater sportsman just about everything there is in the way of affordable electronics for navigating and finding fish. The line of quality products includes: Loran-C receivers, amber and color video depth sounders, chart recorders, LCD depth sounders, digital depth sounders, fixed and hand-held VHF/FM radiotelephones, satellite navigators, electronic charting systems and marine stereos.

One of America's "big three" in brand name recognition of marine electronic products, SI-TEX entered the U.S. market in 1975 as the North American Marine Division of Smiths Industries, Ltd., London, England. In 1988 SI-TEX was purchased by a large Japanese marine electronics manufacturer established in 1947.

In the beginning, SI-TEX products were designed for and sold to commercial fishermen. As the physical size and monetary cost of marine electronic products gradually reduced, SI-TEX began to introduce commercial grade-fishing electronics into the consumer market at affordable prices. Today the majority of SI-TEX products are sold to dedicated saltwater sportsmen who have high performance demands and limited mounting space on their boats.

Leading the way in the integration of instruments for these boats, SI-TEX has been the first and only company to introduce a combination color video depth sounder, Loran-C receiver and XY-axis video plotter in one space saving package.

SI-TEX's Customer Service Department is open from 8:30 to 4:30 Monday through Friday to answer any questions about your SI-TEX equipment. Just call 813-535-4681 and a customer service representative will be happy to assist you.

THE OUT ISLANDS OF THE BAHAMAS

The Commonwealth of The Bahamas consists of some seven hundred (700) islands and nearly 2,500 small islets or cays. Of the roughly 30 inhabited islands, the two major population centres are the capital city of Nassau, on the island of New Providence and Freeport, on the island of Grand Bahama. The other populated islands and cays are known collectively as the Out Islands, the major ones being Abaco, Andros, the Berry Islands, Bimini, Cat Island, Crooked Island, Eleuthera, Exuma, Harbour Island, Long Island, San Salvador and Spanish Wells.

Among the Out Islands are found every imaginable type of tropical setting. Deserted slivers of shimmering white and pink sand, rocky cliffs shaped by Atlantic swells, quiet coves, bustling harbours and quaint towns that look like New England seacoast villages that someone splashed with pastel. And then there's the water, always crystal clear but with ever changing hues from cobalt to electric blue to pale bottle green laced with reefs for exploring and populated by every imaginable game fish. The Out Islands is home to the Bahamas largest island – Andros, and the highest point in The Bahamas, the 206 ft. 'peak' of Cat Island.

EVINRUDE . . . First in Outboards

Since Ole Evinrude first invented the outboard motor back in 1909, Evinrude outboards have continually been on the leading edge of technology and design, providing the ultimate in consumer features and benefits. The company was originally formed as the Evinrude Motor Company, but in the late 1920's, it also established the ELTO Motor Company. E.L.T.O. was the abbreviation for Evinrude Light Twin Outboard.

The early motors were either single or twin cylinder, but in 1928, ELTO introduced the ELTO Quad, the first 4-cylinder engine. Four-cylinder technology continued into the 1950's, culminating with the Evinrude Starflight V-4 50 HP, the first V-4 engine. High tech V-4 and V-6 engines today are loop charged and utilize advanced manufacturing techniques such as lost foam die casting, which allows for much more design detail and eliminates many additional parts such as water cover jackets.

Engine development continues at Evinrude with features such as Quik Start electronic engine control system, which increases idle speed automatically until engine temperature reaches normal operating range and VRO^2, the only oil injection system that sounds an alarm when there is no oil in the fuel mix. Evinrude is first in Power Steering and Counter-Rotation, offering dual engine rigs in V-8, V-6, and V-4.

The company continues to maintain a long-standing association with conservation groups, fishing tournaments, and outdoor writers, contributing both money and talent to worthwhile projects.

MAKO MARINE INTERNATIONAL

More than 20 years have passed since Mako Marine invaded the offshore world of the large sportfishing boats, opening new horizons for multitudes of anglers. Quality, design, and fishability were the founding principles of Mako and these three factors remain the cornerstone of the company today. They have never forgotten their original philosophy of building the finest fishing boat possible for the serious angler and his family. Regardless of the type of fishing you do, Mako has a model for you, from inshore flats to offshore canyons and everything in between.

There are currently 18 models from 17 to 28 feet in outboard, inboard, and full transom. Center consoles are the mainstay of Mako production, but they also produce family cabin and walk-around designs. In the near future, you will see even more growth and expansion at Mako Marine.

Fishing is a way of life at Mako and their Owners' Tournaments (started back in 1970 and now called "Funaments") span the waterfront from Massachusetts to Key West and Texas to Michigan. There are more than 30 scheduled for 1994 including one on Grand Cayman Island for marlin. Each Funament is family fun, release oriented, and based on the honor system, so everybody wins.

Mako believes in marine conservation, fostering the release of fish and supporting organizations working to protect our precious natural resources. They ask you to do the same, because the future of fishing depends on it. Mako Marine is proud to be a part of the Salt Water Sportsman National Seminar Series.

If you would like more information on Mako, write them at Mako Marine, Inc., 4355 N.W. 128th Street, Miami, Florida 33054 or call (305) 685-6591.

CAPT. HARRY'S FISHING SUPPLY

Capt. Harry's customers don't just "go fishin'," they "go catchin'"! Experience 25 years of knowledge and experience, free for the asking, right from your own living room. There are great prices and service to go along with all of this too. Whether it is over the counter or on the telephone, Capt. Harry's staff is going to help answer even your most difficult fishing question.

Why do we share our knowledge and experience with our customers? Because we believe "Catchin'" is what makes fishing so enjoyable. Our knowledge and experience is not just limited to the United States. Our catalog sales currently reach 160 countries providing us with a worldwide network of information for all of our customers

So remember, the next time you are planning a fishing trip…whether it's Baja, Islamorada, or your own backyard, discover the secret that professional fishermen have known for years. Most people go fishing, but the people who shop at Capt. Harry's Fishing Supply "Go Catchin.'"

PENN REELS: The Great American Tackle Company

In 1932, on the third floor of an old North Philadelphia factory, a young German immigrant with a genius for engineering and the determination never to compromise on quality developed a better way to make fishing reels with a drag that outperformed all others. Otto Henze founded Penn Reels on the credo: "Make it simple, make it work." For more than half a century, Penn has followed that philosophy that vaulted them to a leadership role in major angling achievements around the world. More records have been set on Penn tackle than all other makes combined.

Rugged performance coupled with innovative features have characterized Penn reels over the decades. In the 1940's, Otto Henze introduced the levelwinds; by 1950, Penn had worldwide distribution with parts and service available anywhere. The famous Penn Internationals were the highlight of the 1960's along with spinning reels that carried through the '70's. Today, Penn is becoming an important rod manufacturer with models tailored to many of the 150 reel designs currently in the line.

Penn's dominant position in the fishing industry does not only center on its products. The company has always supported marine conservation and restoration projects of aquatic environments. They continue to stress the release of fish and protection of habitat.

In product, philosophy, and practice, Penn earns the title of The Great American Tackle Company day after day, and year after year.

VOLVO PENTA OF THE AMERICAS

Quality comes by design to our motorcars. A legend in precision engineering and craftsmanship, Volvo® represents the ultimate expression of dependable performance to motorists throughout the world. The same dedication to design perfection and attention to manufacturing detail makes Volvo Penta marine power systems the number one choice of experienced boaters. Volvo Penta diesel sterndrives offer the ultimate in performance, reliability and economy. When you know more about marine power you will specify Volvo Penta diesels.

EAGLE CLAW®

Skilled anglers Stan Wright and Drew McGill formed the Wright and McGill Co. in 1925 to produce top quality fishing flies. While fishing for trout on the Colorado River, they watched an Eagle grab a fish. After this observation, they immediately decided to develop a hook with more penetrating power patterned after the bird's talons. Eagle Claw hooks vaulted the company into North America's largest fishhook manufacturer, which now offers several thousand styles and sizes. In order to enhance all saltwater fishing situations, Eagle Claw has developed a revolutionary, long lasting finish for their ocean hooks, which is known as SeaGuard™. The SeaGuard finish has been thoroughly tested by the ASTM-B 117 Salt Spray Corrosion Standards. The results were that SeaGuard lasted 120 hours before the first signs of general rust were visible. This is 40% longer than any competitors comparable hooks.

Eagle Claw offers a variety of saltwater styles and sizes for the following species: **Billfish:** CM1015, CM1020, CM1030, CM1040, CM1050, CM1060, CM1061, CM1070, LE9011, LE9016, LE9014, LE9015, LE9018, LE9021. **Blackfish:** 9100. **Bluefish:** 250, 250H, 9340, 9380. **Codfish:** 165, L197, 9200. **Dolphin:** L317MG, L318N, CM1080. **Flounder:** L134, 9160. **Fluke:** L146, L197, 9144, 9146. **Halibut:** 190. **King Mackerel:** 108, L118, 774. **Mackerel:** 108. **Redfish:** L146, L197, 677. **Shark:** CM1060, CM1070, LE9021. **Snook:** L146, L197, 254SS. **Striped Bass:** 165, 188, L197, CM1080, 9212, 9214. **Tarpon:** 190. **Tuna:** L116MG, L118MG, L317MG, L318N, CM1080, LE9011. **Wahoo:** CM1010, CM1015, CM1020, CM1030.

NOW EAGLE CLAW HAS OCEANS OF NEW SALTWATER TACKLE.

Eagle Claw, the name that has meant game fish hooks since 1925, is introducing a complete new line of saltwater tackle. They feature rust resistant Sea Guard™ finish, extra tough and strong high carbon steel and Lazer Sharp® points.

The line includes a wide variety of styles and sizes, snelled hooks, Comstock rigs...even trebles.

You will find them at your favorite tackle shop today!

EAGLE CLAW®

WRIGHT & McGILL CO • DENVER, COLORADO • 80216 • U.S.A.

A Very Important Message From
ANDE Monofilament

This discarded line is done fishing. But it's not done killing.

Each year we ship thousands of miles of fishing line to anglers all over the world. Unfortunately, when this line is put on the reel the old line comes off or yards are cut off to eliminate frays or nicks. This old line is a deadly killer to all marine life unless it is properly disposed of.

Carelessly discarded plastic fishing line can keep working long after you're done with it — entangling birds, seals, sea turtles, and other animals.

And because plastic line is strong and durable, it's nearly impossible for these animals to break free. They strangle, drown, or starve. That's not sporting.

Some birds even use old fishing line in their nests, creating death traps for their young.

Other plastic debris can be dangerous, too. Fish, birds and seals become entangled in six-pack rings. Sea turtles eat plastic bags—which they mistake for jellyfish—and suffer internal injury, intestinal blockage, or death by starvation. Birds are known to ingest everything from small plastic pieces to plastic cigarette lighters and bottle caps.

Plastic debris also can foul boat propellers and block cooling intakes, causing annoying— sometimes dangerous— delays and causing costly repairs.

So please, save your old fishing line and other plastic trash for proper disposal.

That's not all you'll be saving.

All of us at ANDE thank you for reading the above, and hope you will join in making our waterways safe from old monofilament. We "all" can make a real difference.

ANDE®
MONOFILAMENT

MORE THAN 400 CURRENT
IGFA WORLD RECORDS.
1310 53rd Street
West Palm Beach, FL 33407
(407) 842-2474

Hope Town, Abaco

F.Y.I. CANDICE BERGEN SPOTTED
IN ABACO

No Executive Producers

No Secretaries

No Matching Blazers

No Secretaries

No Vice Presidentes

No Secretaries

THE ISLANDS OF THE BAHAMAS

It Just Keeps Getting Better

Call your travel agent · http://www.interknowledge.com/bahamas

Peace & Plenty
Bonefish Lodge, Ltd.

FOR RESERVATIONS, CALL: (809) 345-5555, OR WRITE:
PEACE & PLENTY BONEFISH LODGE
POST OFFICE BOX 29173
GEORGE TOWN, GREAT EXUMA
THE BAHAMAS

Hit More Tuna And Blues With A Cannon.

Whether you're in the canyons for tuna or in-shore for blues, Cannon downriggers will put you on more fish.

Many a successful day fishing has come from conventional rigs, but Cannon downriggers added to your typical set will improve your hit rate. Tuna and blues spend more time below the surface than at it so it only makes sense to put some of your baits right in front of their noses.

The Cannon Marlin Electric HP™ or Uni-Troll HP™ are just the answers to lower your baits and raise your catch rate. No wire line, no heavy weights to fight, just hard-fighting fish.

The Marlin Electric HP or Uni-Troll HP are made to take the tough conditions saltwater fishing dishes out. From the tough Lexan body to anti-corrosive fittings and connectors, the Marlin Electric HP and Uni-Troll HP are built to last season after season.

The Marlin Electric HP offers the fastest electric drive on the market. The Uni-Troll HP also offers a 50 percent faster retrieve ratio. That means a lot when you are setting lines when the bite is on. Both come with a telescoping boom that extends from two to five feet and any length in between to meet your particular needs.

Couple downrigger run baits with your surface baits and we're betting that your success rates improve.

Check out the Cannon Marlin Electric HP or Uni-Troll HP at your nearest authorized Cannon dealer, or write for our new product catalog. And for 16 pages of fish-catching tips, get Cannon's *Guide to Saltwater Fishing with Downriggers.* Just send $5.99 to Computrol/Cannon, 499 East Corporate Dr., Meridian, Idaho 33642.

CANNON

HIT MORE FISH WITH A CANNON

MAKO IS PROUD TO BE PART OF THE
NINETH SALT WATER SPORTSMAN NATIONAL SEMINAR SERIES
FOR 1996

There is one boat and one boat company that has stood for quality and value for 25 years. Their management has always been dedicated to building the finest fishing boat. Their dealer network is outstanding. Their consumer acceptance and loyalty is unsurpassed. They hold more owner, "family" fishing tournaments than all of their competition combined. The resale value of their boat is the highest and their design, innovations, and fishability are the benchmark for others to try to follow. So, in the world of sportfishing, one name has always stood above the rest. The name is Mako, the reason is quality. If you're looking for the best, there isn't much else on the horizon. Mako…You'll find them where the fish are.

MAKO MARINE
INTERNATIONAL
4355 Northwest 128th Street, Miami, Florida 33054

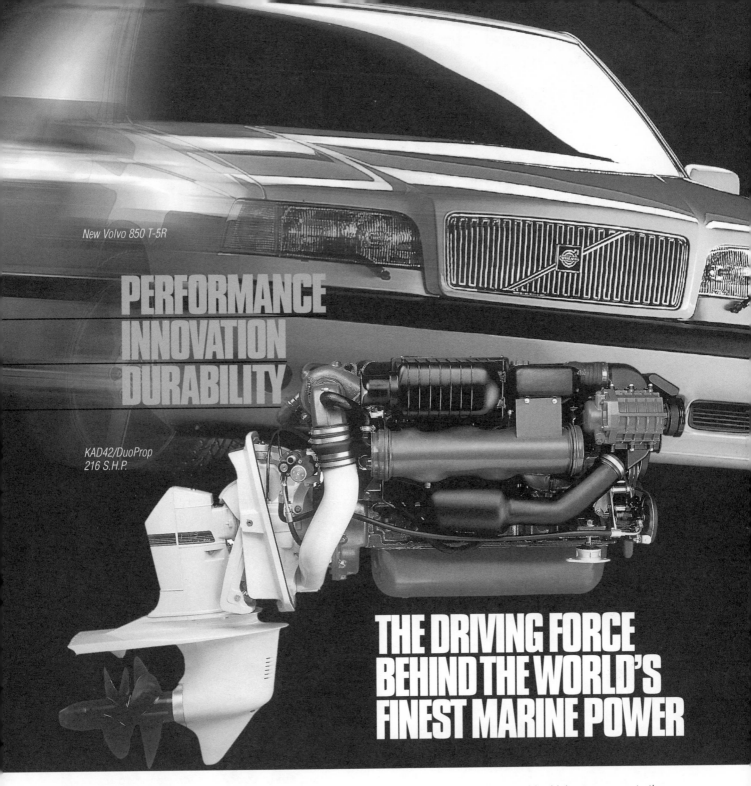

New Volvo 850 T-5R

PERFORMANCE INNOVATION DURABILITY

KAD42/DuoProp
216 S.H.P.

THE DRIVING FORCE BEHIND THE WORLD'S FINEST MARINE POWER

Quality comes by design to our motorcars. A legend in precision engineering and craftsmanship, Volvo® represents the ultimate expression of dependable performance to motorists throughout the world. The same dedication to design perfection and attention to manufacturing detail makes Volvo Penta marine power systems the number one choice of experienced boaters. Volvo Penta diesel sterndrives offer the ultimate in performance, reliability and economy. When you know more about marine power you will specify Volvo Penta diesels.

VOLVO PENTA®

For a free catalog and the
name of your nearest dealer,
call **1-800-525-5508**

WHEN YOU KNOW MORE
ABOUT MARINE POWER

EVINRUDE OCEANPRO™ OUTBOARDS

WHAT SETS THEM APART IS HOW WE PUT THEM TOGETHER.

Patented state-of-the-art technology. Strict manufacturing processes. And the most comprehensive system of corrosion protection ever devised. That's what Evinrude incorporates into these V6s, and what makes them the only true 200 and 225 HP saltwater outboards.

Only Evinrude OceanPro™ outboards offer a stainless steel steering arm and pivot shaft.

We start by using *more stainless steel*—in more components—than any competitive outboard. Then we add EDP coatings, our 13-step Deep Guard™ process and high temperature silicone paints. And with our freshwater flushing port and patented relieved split-line gearcase—it's the best anti-corrosion system ever devised.

Yet, corrosion resistance is hardly the only thing that distinguishes these loop-charged outboards. Finger port cylinders deliver blistering acceleration and unbeatable fuel economy. Our innovative closed-deck powerhead combines superior power with quiet operation. For reliability, Evinrude OceanPro™ outboards are unrivaled, thanks to half-keystone piston rings and a lost-foam cast block.

Our freshwater flushing port lets you flush out harmful saltwater without running the engine.

MORE STAINLESS STEEL

More corrosion fighting stainless steel than any competitive outboard.

The finger port cylinders combine greater low-end power with exceptional fuel economy.

Unwavering reliability, awesome power and superior corrosion resistance. It not only sets these Evinrude OceanPro™ V6s apart from the competition, it takes them far beyond. Check them out at your Evinrude dealer today.

For more information and the location of your nearby Evinrude dealer call:

1-800-998-9960

EVINRUDE⋐
OUTBOARDS
LEADING THE WAY™

TO BUILD THE DEFINITIVE SALTWATER V4, WE TOOK A LOOK AT THE ULTIMATE V6.

INTRODUCING THE NEW JOHNSON OCEANRUNNER® V4'S.

Once you've built the most advanced V6 saltwater outboard ever conceived, it's easy to build the ultimate saltwater V4. In fact, our new 90 and 115 HP V4's offer all the advanced technology made famous by our OceanRunner 150 and 175 HP V6's. To fight corrosion, we employ *more stainless* **MORE STAINLESS STEEL** *steel* than any other outboard. With EDP coatings, high-temperature silicone paints, and our Deep Guard™ process, it's simply the most extensive corrosion protection system you can get. For performance—finger port cylinder sleeves, Power Path™ induction and a closed-deck powerhead combine blistering acceleration with exceptional fuel economy. And with our unique vapor separator and the infrared technology of our OIS 2000™ Optical Ignition System, no outboard is more reliable or efficient. The Johnson® OceanRunner V6 has finally met its match... the new OceanRunner V4's.

Exclusive!
Only OceanRunner outboards feature a stainless steel steering arm and pivot shaft.

For more information and the location of your nearby Johnson dealer, call: *1-800-998-9960*

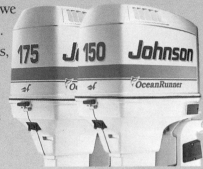

Our V6 technology established benchmarks for performance and corrosion resistance in offshore outboards. You'll find all that same technology in our new V4's.

Exclusive!
Our OIS 2000™ Optical Ignition System assures precise engine timing.

Exclusive!
Our unique vapor separator virtually ends starting problems caused by vapor lock.

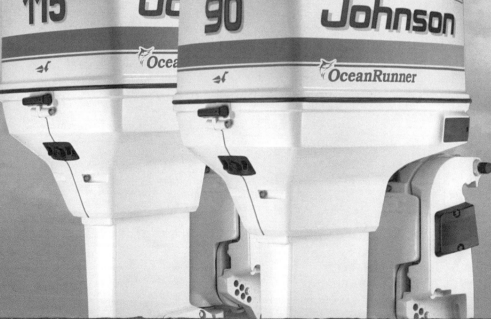

The Power of Experience™

THE SUN NEVER SETS AT CAPT. HARRY'S FISHING SUPPLY.

We are a full-service fishing and tackle outfit, and what separates us from the rest is our 26-year old reputation, talented staff and customer service...That would make us the most complete fishing shop in the FLORIDA region.

We specialize in over 20,000 fishing related products. We have the best selection of saltwater rods, reels, terminal tackle, lures, flies, fly fishing equipment, fly tying materials, clothing, gifts and more. Whether you are deep sea fishing, light tackle or fly fishing, we can offer suggestions.

We are thrilled about our newly expanded 96-page catalog. We have filled these pages with exciting new products. We have increased our selection of clothing, and have expanded our women's and kids' categories. We have developed a line of ceramic gifts that include a decanter set, lamps, mugs, platters and more. Each one of these gift items include a variety of specially designed hand-painted fish motifs that are personally signed by the artist.

We also must mention, that we have increased the size of our retail location. We would like to invite you to stop by our Miami store and introduce yourselves, or call us directly TOLL-FREE 1-800-327-4088, and allow our staff to service all of your needs. We look forward to hearing from you.

So the next time you are planning your fishing trip and need some expertise, remember a couple of important things. "A lot of people go fishing, but the people who shop at Capt. Harry's Fishing Supply 'Go Catchin'.

Good Fishing "Catchin'"

CALL FOR FREE CATALOG

Capt. Harry's FISHING SUPPLY
ORDER TOLL-FREE
24 HOURS-A-DAY
1-800-327-4088
DEPT. SSS

Dept. SSS • 100 N.E. 11th Street • Miami, Florida 33132 • Phone: 305-374-4661 • Fax: 305-374-3713

W O R L D W I D E   S E R V I C E

Sperry Top-Sider® is proud to

support the 1996 Saltwater

Sportsman National Seminar

Series. Stop by our display to

When you know the water.™

see a wide selection of Sperry

Top-Sider® footwear, includ-

ing the revolutionary new

SB770 ~ the lightest weight

marine athletic shoe ever.

Isles And Isles To Choose From.

The Most Service To The Most Caribbean Isles.

If you're shopping around for the perfect Caribbean or Bahamas vacation, try us on for size.
Because only American Airlines and American Eagle® can take you to 35 destinations on 26 islands.
That means more sailing, dining, nightlife and, of course, shopping than anyone else can give you. What's
even better is we offer exciting and affordable Fly AAway Vacations® packages to most of these tropical
islands. Call your Travel Agent or American at **1-800-624-6262** today. And do a little browsing.

AmericanAirlines®
American *Eagle*®